My Dear Alexias

My Dear Alexias

Letters
from
Wellesley Tudor Pole
to
Rosamond Lehmann

Edited by
Elizabeth Gaythorpe
With a Foreword by
Rosamond Lehmann

JERSEY
NEVILLE SPEARMAN

First published in Great Britain 1979 by
Neville Spearman (Jersey) Ltd
PO Box 75, Normandy House, St. Helier, Jersey
Channel Islands

Distributed by Neville Spearman Ltd
The Priory Gate, Friars Street, Sudbury, Suffolk

© Rosamond Lehmann 1979

ISBN 0 85978 038 4

Text set in 10/12 pt Times Roman by
Galleon Photosetting, Ipswich
and printed and bound by
Billing & Sons Ltd, Guildford

Foreword

Wellesley Tudor Pole as I knew him

In introducing a selection of the many letters written to me by Wellesley Tudor Pole between 1963 and 1968 – (the year of his final withdrawal, to use a term he favoured) – I am not venturing on a full account of his long life, or attempting a full appraisal of his work. Indeed, the task would be impossible: for one thing, he destroyed all the hundreds of letters he received; for another, although there is no doubt of the impact he made upon the history of our times, his great mission was anonymous and secret. So this brief memoir is a personal one.

Who was the well-loved, highly respected person known to many as TP – and moreover thus referred to by himself: as if someone speaking from another viewpoint were observing and commenting upon a quite separate individual? Needless to say, I am not describing a schizoid split in personality: most of us, I think, are aware of a detached interior watcher in times of acute physical or emotional stress; but TP quite often wrote as if his Ego was aware of having temporarily adopted a separate vehicle – one with which he did not always altogether feel at home.

Who was he? Who was he *really*? I do not know. No one in his last life knew for certain – except, presumably, certain Elder Brothers and fellow-Initiates in incarnation. 'We carry a light, you know,' he said to me once. 'That's how we recognize each other.' And various passages in his letters hint at the same mystery. For instance: 'No peace on earth for this Wicked One, whose identity is fortunately unknown and unrecognized, this being perhaps TP's

1

only worthwhile achievement during his present sojourn.' And again: 'I am a modest and anonymous ambassador from elsewhere. . . .' 'The human race is not my race. . . .' 'This is not my planet.' Once he said: 'I'm a rough sort of fellow, very rough: not a polished, sophisticated social asset. I've got a frightful temper, it would shock you.' But once only did I witness it, and then it seemed a transpersonal outburst, a solemn rebuke to mere curiosity; a warning to dabblers in the occult. (I'm thankful to say that I was not the culprit). For the rest, he loved to tease, and now and then he spiced his letters with a cryptic, tantalizing 'lead'. And then I *was* tempted to probe further; but, deliberately, I never did. Yet I wonder now whether in fact he could have been telling me he trusted me to take another step . . . and see what came of it.

I first met him early in 1963; and it was my great privilege to become his close friend and collaborator during his last six years. My path crossed his at a time when I was struggling, not very successfully, to recover from a shattering bereavement. He gave me fresh hope and courage, warm yet astringent sympathy. Above all, he gave me the solid metaphysical grounding which I was seeking and had always lacked. It was an immense privilege to be of service to him as 'a sort of anvil on which he could strike sparks that would help him to recover clarity of vision'; or so he says in his Foreword to *A Man Seen Afar* – the book I edited for him. I fear that the anvil rings less brightly now than it did then, when I was under his discipline: harnessed, he called it, to his dynamo. He made a courteous if not very plausible show of deploring the demands he made upon my time and energy; of apologizing for his constant exhortations to wake up and stretch my own dormant faculties. I knew the idea was to spur me on to subordinate any work of mine to his.

He was full of wit, and loved to laugh, and we shared many jokes – and this was good for him as well as for me. He believed in the importance of laughter as a catalyst, for his life was incredibly arduous by day and by night; and although his temperament was sanguine he was sometimes exhausted, frustrated and despondent. I still remember his amusement when I told him that our meeting had been foretold by a numerologist at the College of Psychic Studies' Christmas Fair in 1962. A gentleman, she told me, about seventy-eight years old, was shortly coming my way and would change my life. Elderly gentlemen, did not I agree, could be such wonderful companions? Dubiously and with strong if tacit reservations, I agreed. This was a story he particularly relished – pressing me to admit that it had been a spot-on prediction.

When I first came face to face with him, which was over coffee in the St. Ermin's Hotel, I experienced a distinct sense of shock. I don't know if this was due to some subconscious stir of recognition, or to a deeper, one might say spiritual malaise. I was in the presence of someone quite formidably *awake*; and my nerve ends got the message which his old-fashioned courtesy and shield of banter tried to mask. Then and later he gave me a sense . . . a tingling electric sense, as of being lightly showered with fiery particles – and sometimes lightly stung by them. Later he dropped the banter; but I noticed it was an armour he was apt to reassume in unfamiliar company. It could be disconcerting – Puckish. Indeed there *was* a strong element of the devic in his make-up: his love of trees was passionate, and he seemed able to communicate wordlessly with each and all of the seven kingdoms of Nature. It was not difficult to see him as an alchemist, or as a practitioner of white magic, particularly in relation to herbal remedies and nature cure in general. And he was warning of the disastrous threat of planetary pollution at least thirty years before this became a matter of public concern.

TP was a very proud man, and a shy one; and after the death in the early fifties of his beloved wife, lonely in his domestic life. (By then his daughter and his two sons were married, with homes and families of their own; and I very rarely had the pleasure of meeting them.) He and his sister Katharine were devotedly attached. Now in her mid-nineties, she is a remarkable and delightful lady, whom I hope and believe I may consider as a friend. They both set store by their distinguished Tudor and Pole ancestry; and had inherited dark Celtic looks and fine bone structure. In addition, TP was the possessor of an exceptionally attractive speaking voice – strong, vibrant, musical.

He could be caustic, even imperious, like one accustomed to command and to be obeyed; at the same time he radiated benevolence and charm, as well as genuine humility of spirit. Above all, he radiated *sanity*. What he most abhorred was humbug, sanctimoniousness – anything smacking of cant or 'uplift'. While scrupulous to respect the 'path' of every seeker, he was impatient of doctrinaire rigidity and dogma. He had old-fashioned moral standards of behaviour, and might even have been thought prudish. Yet his charity towards 'sinners' was boundless.

He really did change some people's lives radically for the better, by some occult process of re-harmonization, of spiritual alchemy. The gifts he gave so generously, so unobtrusively, were beyond price; yet he told me more than once that he looked back on his long life with a sense of failure: he had, he said, missed so many opportunities of service.

While he still kept a London office, from which he controlled family business interests and Chalice Well Trust and other practical affairs, I saw him chiefly in London. But during his latter years of failing health and eyesight I would drive down as often as I could to Hurstpierpoint to spend a few hours with him. His house was a modest one (bought after the destruction by bombing of his London home), semi-detached, with a plot of front lawn, and rose beds, and a neat little living room like a Victorian parlour. Here he lived frugally, ruled by an elderly housekeeper, who concealed her genuine devotion beneath a rebarbative exterior; and by a noisy tyrannical old Corgi called Kipps. One went up steep stairs to the tiny attic sanctuary where a silver hanging lamp of oriental design perpetually shone; and where the wondrous mysterious sapphire bowl reposed in its casket of carved olive wood. There was an indescribable peace, a sense of beneficent Presence in that sanctuary. Now and then he wrote of expecting or of entertaining this or that visitor – quite a stream of visitors, sometimes from overseas; but I always saw him alone. I have since asked myself if a proportion, at least, of these visitors could have been discarnate.

He carried on an immense, a global, correspondence: he told me he wrote at least two hundred letters every week: I am sure this was no exaggeration. To me he wrote, sometimes at considerable length, two or three times a week. How I welcomed the coming of those bulky envelopes, inscribed in his uniquely large and legible handwriting! Owing to Elizabeth Gaythorpe's invaluable editorial assistance I am at last able to present the major part of their contents, and to feel I have discharged some portion of my debt to the dearly loved friend to whom I was 'Alexias', from the first.

4

I am not of course suggesting that I was the only person to whom he confided matters of importance, or the only one who valued his letters sufficiently to keep them. I believe that, for instance, he wrote daily to a friend of his youth during World War I when he served as an officer in Military Intelligence; and that trunksful of these letters are stored in the care of this friend's son, Sir David Russell, TP's godson. Surely these would repay investigation.

If only I had realized that his time on earth was fast running out, I would have stayed nearer to TP during that last summer. But I did not realize it, and went abroad for three weeks; and by the time I came back his condition had shockingly deteriorated. Strangely enough, for a person so profoundly aware, he seemed not to have accepted his imminent departure, and said to me that he had left certain tasks unfinished, and that he would be granted 'an extension' before obtaining his order of release. But his frail body, which for two years at least had endured bouts of atrocious pain with scarcely a murmur of complaint, was breaking down too irretrievably to contain his spirit any longer. I was by his bedside three times during the final fortnight. It was a cruelly hard death, and agonizing to watch for those who cherished him. Maybe great souls willingly assume a portion of the world's suffering at the time of their departure. At least, he once told me so, speaking of Pope John. I do not doubt that he was of their company.

I want to stress my indebtedness to my friend Elizabeth Gaythorpe for her splendid work on the mass of material with which I burdened her. Possessing neither her orderly mind nor her typing skill, I dreaded undertaking the task of editorship myself. Besides, it seemed too troubling an assignment. Although I am still able (by courtesy of Cynthia Sandys) to be in touch with him from time to time (see the section called the Glastonbury Scripts in *The Awakening Letters*) his going has deprived me of a kind of nourishment, a daily bread upon which I had come to rely – I fear perhaps to take too much for granted. Alas, one *is* inclined to take constant affection and concern too much for granted while the atmosphere of warmth and happiness they generate is still around one like a soothing vitalizing bath. But gratitude – and more than that, a sense of awe when I consider certain insights and illuminations he permitted me to share with him: these grow stronger as the years go on. My sincere thanks are also due to Neville

Well the first and not unimportant problem is the question of names. What in fact shall we call each other? Destiny can play ironical tricks when it so desires. Although you and I have shared, enjoyed, suffered, endured many experiences together in the past; there has been so much needless delay in our crossing each other's paths during our present incarnations. What a pity, when so much awaits exchanging and renewing.

I am not much good at remembering names but I fancy that Alexias of Greek times, written about in some of Mary Renault's books, bears a strong resemblance to the character and make up of the present Rosamond Lehmann. Therefore, subject to your gracious and willing permission may I call you Alexias? Or would you prefer a name from earlier times in Egypt, Persia or the Far East? As to WTP, most people call me TP (*tout court*) and it serves for those who care not for Wellesley.

I have just been spending hours and hours in writing letters to people appealing for advice who seem to think I am a man of huge leisure, at everyone's beck and call. It comes as a relief to share a few thoughts and feelings with you: remember however that I come of a rather ferocious stock.

My forebear Owen, enraged at the conquest of Wales, enticed King Henry's widow to his bed in revenge. Ultimately marrying her and starting the Tudor dynasty. We always have a Tudor and a Katharine in each of our family's generations. Well, we Tudors with all our wickedness have now become a part of England and on my Father's side we have a Cardinal who lost his head, and a Norman origin through the de la Poles. And I was born on St. George's Day which was also the anniversary of Shakespeare's birth and death. And so, although my present work is mainly international, I am still a part of England and proud of it. Owen Tudor of course was descended from the line of the King Arthurs and back from there to the Royal line of Israel and behind that Assyria. *Now* you will see how necessary it is for you not to tread too heavily upon my royal corns.

Yes I love the mellow Rhine and Rhone wines but I care not for spirits. Nor do I eat fish, flesh or fowl. What more can I tell you? I was happily married for forty years to a very lovely and understanding lady. And since 1952 I have been refusing matrimony regularly and frequently. Now at ninety-nine* I await my call and am ready to go, so soon as Destiny will allow it to come about.

Now fair is fair and you should tell me something of your own past! Some of which I know.

I am asked by a correspondent if I realize the significance of the fact that Leonardo da Vinci's mother was a barmaid.

What is he driving at? I daresay most of us descend from barmaids in one way or another, usually nice buxom creatures full of health and good spirits. In my view just as good a forebear as a carpenter (or a beheaded Cardinal).

No more nonsense from me today.

24.1.63

In accordance with Your Majesty's commands I have contacted T.E.L. and this is his response.

'I am not aware of communicating through either my Ross or Shaw personalities. But this is not surprising seeing that I am still trying to combine my three earthly personalities in a unity, through which I hope in time to reach my true and lasting individuality.'

The above is an interpretation *in words* of the ideas expressed to WTP by T.E.L.

Never fear! The spate of letters will soon ease off. I am only trying to make up for much needless loss of time by bringing you up to date. And whilst I am still here. However, if you *will* link yourself to the TP dynamo, then say good-bye to any peaceful leisure.

* A joke, of course.

Yes Lawrence feared the ladies but *who doesn't?* with their magnetic allure and their peculiar ways (this of course does not refer to Alexias). Incarnations – yes some time, but why disturb more emotional vibrations from the past?

Of course you *would* be born during a thunderstorm! Once you arrived down here when the earth shook. My dear and faithful one was also born on the day you name. WTP came along on the 23rd April 1884, around 3 p.m.

26.1.63

What a lot of elementary dope I have written over the years! When I happen to re-read it I am filled with consternation for its inadequacy. Can such writings do *any* good? The enclosed for instance, who will heed or believe its contents, so clumsy and so poorly written. Tell me very frankly some time whether my sort of elementary writings are of any value at all to anyone? In my moments I doubt it.

Do not trouble to return this leaflet. It can be turned into spills for lighting fires. Or don't you have open grates?

One day years and years ago I was sitting in the walled garden of a Stamboul inn, drinking ânak with a group of young Turks. It was a cold night and we had a charcoal brazier brought out and placed near our table. Then hot black sweet Turkish coffee was served and as guest of honour I was given the first cup to drink. I put it to my lips but did not drink. One of my hosts sitting on my right then drank his cup and fell dead at our feet. Immediately the man next to him swept the tray of cups and coffee to the ground. And then they all jumped away into the darkness of the night.

They were Atatürk's 'Young Turks' and the year was 1908, early Spring.

It was the Sultan's spies who had bribed the innkeeper and served the coffee themselves. In those days WTP bore a charmed life: knives, poison, drowning, lure of the harems – none of these seemed capable of finishing him off. And it was the same in war and in revolution. I did not deserve my luck for I was a very ordinary person. It was the mention of coal fires that brought this incident back into memory.

I cannot write my own life story, nor would wish to do so; but there is enough material to make the sort of book that people like to read. Try your hand at it?!!! Once my very carefully fixed and tended beard fell into my soup when dining on the Orient Express in full view. That shows you what a priceless idiot I can be on occasion.

Well now I have brought you up to date sufficiently for a *re*-linking that will survive our present lives. Invite yourself any Wednesday or Friday to coffee or liqueur around 2.15 p.m. Don't stand on ceremony. I spoke of time being short, perhaps. Last June I was in Czechoslovakia, I expect a 'call' into Russia this coming summer and I hardly expect to return. I cannot refuse. Meanwhile I have speaking engagements at Coventry, Knutsford, Shrewsbury, Glastonbury, Eastbourne and elsewhere. And loads of clearing the decks, and work. And Etna.

28.1.63

Letters. Usually better destroyed, anyway after a while. They only clutter and go yellow. My correspondence with Walburga Lady Paget, intimate and political, has had a strange destiny. Full of inside stuff about Lloyd George, Curzon, Milner, Balfour, Crookes, Archdeacon Wilberforce, Allenby, Storrs, Lawrence and so on – I asked her to destroy them. But she left them to her daughter Gay (Lady Plymouth), who was a buddy of WTP's, and *she* left them to her daughter Lady Phyllis Bentley. The latter without my consent sold them to the British Museum, and refused to return them to me, saying they were not my property. However I made the B.M. agree not to place them at public disposal before fifty years had passed after Walburga's departure.

Gay was a wayward waif. On one occasion during a ball at their lovely house in Mount Street she took me aside, tore off a string of priceless pearls she was wearing, and thrusting these into my pocket said, 'Windsor keeps me so short of cash. Do get me some with these.' (Windsor – Lord P. – was a millionaire). Somehow I got her to put them on again and then I raced for my life. But she was a dear. Do you like such stories or do they bore you?

12.2.63

What does the N.* stand for? Nimble, notorious, naughty, nonconformist, notable, nippy? Welcome indeed to our Chalice Well Companionship. Come down later on when TP is in residence.

I do realize your keen disappointment and disillusion when told that your next significant contact would be with 'an elderly gentleman'† . . . and now that the honeymoon must be considered over – most pleasant in restrospect – the elderly gentleman will get down to business. Intensive training should now begin as a fresh page starts in A's experiences.

For a start therefore:

1. Summarize in about 100 words why she believes (or otherwise) that the 'saying' on page 9 of the Enigma booklet is true; and if so why?
2. State how she stands in her thinking towards the problem of 'Evil'. Does she believe it to possess entity and intelligence, temporary or otherwise; and if so on what grounds? (Take your time. *Think* very carefully.)

To *remember*: That R.N.L. still has to write a book which will live and inspire, long after the writer has assumed the title 'Queen of Limbo' or (less likely?) Queen of Paradise.

* Reference to my second name, Nina.
† A numerologist–clairvoyant had read my hand at a CPS Christmas bazaar some weeks previously, and 'saw', to my dismay, that my next 'beau' would be a gentleman about eighty years old!

Limbo is the region where dwell souls who are forgotten and who have forgotten themselves.

When you are adequately trained, here is where your services will be called for (I have your own Guardian's consent to this and also Sally's immense but not yet full meed of understanding). But you will have to stand on your own feet in due course, for WTP may be beyond reach for a time, before very long. (You should have contacted your elderly gentleman earlier!)

Daily pray: 'I dedicate myself anew to the service of my Creator and to *all* forms of life upon and around this Planet. Grant me strength, humility and inspiration for these purposes.'

As inner perceptions begin to be aroused, sensitivity increases. One needs to build a mental and emotional protective shield. Go to it as you will need it. As you have guessed my own species of protective shield is a form of seeming flippancy.

A propos. A great lady wrote to give thanks that the Tudors had now produced a 'Saint'. I responded by relating the exploit of my Owen Tudor ancestor vis-*à*-vis Katharine; I went on to tell Her Grace about the more outrageous excesses of my Tudor relations, sexual and political, and ended: 'How on earth can you imagine a Saint flowering on such a stalk?' No doubt I am no longer on her reception list, but *what* a joy to be naughty now and then!

Advice

Now that you are approaching an important cross road in your present life (due as the new Solar Year opens), a measure of stocktaking is necessary. Face yourself frankly. Sit down quietly and ask yourself:

1. Do I know where I am going?
   Or am I tending to drift?
2. Is my purpose for the next span of my life clear?
   If so, be precise.

3. Am I prepared to dedicate my energies, my thoughts, words and deeds to Service? *What* service? To whom?
4. If called upon to do so what am I willing to give up?
   (a) in society and personal affairs.
   (b) in my own interior life.
5. Do I feel able and ready to take a step forward along the Path leading to the first Gateway of Initiation?

Your answers and decisions are for yourself alone. If you feel there is any wrong or misunderstanding towards others, still in suspense, take steps to mend the matter, humbly.

Meanwhile go on *simplifying*, cutting down wasteful activities, stilling your mind, giving thanks and keeping as serene as you can. Remember that progress and evolution never come through strain. One's personal fate is of little importance and need not concern one unduly. Enlightened service to others without desire of reward, is indeed a Pearl of Great Price.

Amen!

Sunday 17.2.63

Have you such a shockingly low opinion of this lowly creature as to think he cannot equip you during your *present* life, to start work in Limbo? Music conceived and built up mentally will be one of your weapons. Ah me! Ah me! We are alive NOW in supersensible realms. Wake up to this realization, like the good girl you can sometimes be.

The 'Masters' who work quietly in our midst deprecate curiosity. They need complete anonymity. How foolish the T.S. and Bailey people are to try to personalize them, giving them this attribute and that. 'Infants in the night' are they, poor dears, spying among the Gods.

To do a certain job I am lying in bed. Perhaps this accounts for a vein of causticacity (is that a word in respectable use?).

Mauve is not your colour or whatever tint your paper was. Shall I pay the bill for a new supply?

To 'romp and play' (within the bounds of seemliness, or thereabouts), is part of spiritual training, although all these deadly serious occult 'Teachers' will disagree most violently. I always learn more when watching the Gods at play than when they are in serious conclave.

20.2.63

Here are some odds and ends:

You can have all TP's scripts at any time, and write a book around them. There is nothing really sensational or new in these writings but there is a mass of them. One would like to reach a more general public than those associated with spiritualism and all the other isms, and written in a way that is not ponderous or didactic. What people like most are personal anecdotes and experiences, and there you could draw me out endlessly, apart from your own wide range of ideas and feelings. Propaganda is anathema or any kind of preaching. Or piety or sanctimony.

Am engaged in guerrilla warfare with my 'Superiors' just now. (I *love* fighting hopeless odds.) It is over the Russian project, as I would prefer to travel normally and 'They' want me to do the job by a process of de- and re-materializing my body, for a few weeks whilst there. I hate artificial methods even if they turn out to be less dangerous.

Home Work: You say you passed on that booklet to a friend. Did you first read it carefully, spot the inaccuracies and point them out to your friend? Or did you simply run through the writing more or less superficially? If so, go down *one* in your class! Great care should always be exercised in matters of this kind. Especially when dealing with those whose finer perceptions have not yet been aroused. Never accept anything metaphysically that does not

14

receive the full imprimatur of your deep perceptions, your reasoning and your intuitive agreement. So be it!

Etna. We must talk. Alas the grape vine has alerted all kinds of people who try to find out when and where I am going.

23.2.63

Very well, Friday March 1st 7 p.m. But *don't* prepare a special meal for me. A simple omelette or macaroni cheese and fruit, no sauces; and do carry on normally for yourself and other guests. Otherwise I am distressed.

And keep free for Paris 29, 30, 31 March. We will chaperone each other in that alarming city. . . .

Lesson for the Day
On Giving Thanks. Do this without fail on all relevant occasions. Before enjoying a morning's hot bath. Before all meals and before receiving guests or setting out to speak or shop. Before going to sleep. Be a child. Say 'thank you Father', just as Jesus did before healing or teaching work.

Install within yourself an attitude of mind of humble gratitude to your Creator for Life, Love, Truth and for the opportunity TO SERVE.

25.2.63

Rather unexpected news. I asked my own 'Sage' to find out from your Guide why the speeding up of your perceptions was not being undertaken at a more leisurely pace.

That TP for one was disinclined to participate in what might be a rushing process.

The reply may take you aback and even surprised me (a little!) –
To A. 'You are being geared up, trained, to undertake a special task, IF you should decide freely so to do.

'A book to appear in the Spring 1964 at a time when it will be needed. TP to give you his unpublished scripts, to be written round and through; and some of them to form an integral portion of the volume. Delay would probably result in TP not being available to you in an advisory capacity.

'Acceptance of this mission is NOT obligatory and refusal would cause you no personal damage.'

Well my dear! *Could* your decks be cleared in time, should you decide to say YES?

The decision must be unforced, uninfluenced by others, and the result of Prayer and Silence.

26.2.63

Subud
The method as practised over here is dangerous, unenlightened and full of pitfalls. I could give you my reasons at length but you have no need for me so to do.

Spotless
We are here to help our fellows by our love, sympathy, understanding. TP for one could not do this fully unless he was covered with as many spots as the proverbial leopard. Therefore my very dear, do not try to wash your own spots away, not at present in any case. Saints secluded have their value, but we wicked ones are not without our uses.

I am never really happy in posh hotels and restaurants, preferring a hole in the wall, where non-meat eaters are not regarded as vermin. Paris and Rome suit me, and also the lovely fruit meals in Saharan oases. I am *not* a civilized person.

16

Bless you, how tiresome TP can be, leaving you so little peace! Always remember that TP claims no authority whatever as a 'Teacher'. Therefore sift all he tells you and select the grain and throw away the chaff. Do the same when confronted with 'messages' from Venusians, Martians, Oracles, Pan, Minerva, Plotinus ad lib including all your Egyptian friends. I don't want to intervene in any way: *you* are master of your own fate and can claim exemption from interference from any quarter.

Venusians
Each planet, including our earth, has within its aura an under-world and several overworlds. When an Elder Brother appears on earth, he has come down through what we call the mental, the astral, and the etheric (Borderland) planes of consciousness.

He needs no materialized chariot or saucer for his manifes-tations. Elder Brothers belonging to other planets act in the same way: if such beings have reason to approach and enter our own earth levels, they don't travel objectively in external space. Such methods do not conform to celestial Law.

I had occasion to write to Geraldine Cummins with news of her beloved Miss Gibbes. As she (G.C.) is so interested in the elasticity of 'Time', I told her about that Restaurant episode. (For after I left you, I went in due course to the Vega just off Leicester Square.)

Seeing that the table I had been asked to sit at, 'unless forestalled', was vacant, I raced over to occupy it, gleeful at having outwitted the prediction. However a couple who had been hanging up their coats came over and turned me off, saying they had already reserved it.

And so I wedged into the only vacant seat at the next table, much to the resentment of three elderly females already there. They regarded me as an intruder and possibly a disturber of their virginal condition: and off they went in about five minutes, leaving me alone. Then a young fellow came in and made straight for my table and sat down. A complete stranger. He gazed at me for a while, and then without preamble begged me to solve a personal problem of his, connected with his study of the Baghavad Gita. I did this for him and then got up and went my way. Nothing sensational, but apparently worth while. Tell G.C. some time that you were told of this incident beforehand.

12.3.63

Very many thanks for these interesting scripts. Comments when I have digested them.

Those who are already released from their earthly bodies and are evolving souls may well visit the etheric counterparts of the moon or the planets. What *we* see in the sky are simply the external reflections of the reality behind. Our earth is no more than that. It is only because of the 'carry over' mould of the mind and its thinking that messages appear to be describing material external happenings elsewhere (e.g. 'we arrived with a bump'). Yes I do think that certain beings from inner spheres do use now and then the cumbersome methods of materialization and manifest via space conditions. They *may* have a worthwhile mission, a warning mission perhaps. I am open minded and *of course* not infallible.

Yes: SHALŌM DŌM is perhaps the most effective mantra for creating peaceful conditions, when properly intoned (either mentally or vocally). I do *not* look upon Your Majesty as being gullible; all I try to do is to render you free from the need to rely 'for truth' upon 'messages' or mediums, by the arousing of your own interior perceptive faculties.

Yes in a certain sense you can claim royal lineage and some day we may talk over those strange times.

I wonder if I should cancel my present plans for end of April and early May; and go on from Paris to Sicily on that quest. A well known specialist said to me: 'Our efforts to tackle most forms of cancer are as ineffectual as trying to exorcise a ghost, which keeps on eluding us'. He spoke more truly than he knew.

S.S.C. Some time ago she apologized for not sending me the carbon copy of her translation to go through, but said that in any case I should be able to have the script, when it had been 'set up'. I have never heard of the author of a book of this kind being prepared to endorse a foreign translation 'blind'. However, life is short and I have no intention of holding publication up, so long as clause 5 of my contract is honoured. *A quoi bon?* Let us enjoy our stay in Paris without complications or contretemps.

I do not remember meeting Lady Sandys, but to do so under your auspices would indeed be worth while and pleasurable.

I do hope that the sea air has blown all the cobwebs away. I am distressed for *your* distress over your friends' illusions. Sad, because *some* truth is mixed up with them. I am not denying the phenomena associated with Sauceritis but you see, all this turning outwardly to the material skies largely undoes all one's efforts to turn people to seek salvation and spiritual satisfaction *within*.

Some people even believe that so soon as they are 'dead' they at once take forms that enable them to go and live on other planets, *three*-dimensionally! What shocks await even those who think they know all about the next world, and the next but one, and so on. You have your hands full in writing your new book.

And now to S.S.C. The paged budget sent me is said to have been corrected for the Press by her and *finally passed* for printers. I have not dared tell Spearman of the breaking of Clause 5 of their contract. Originally S.S.C.* agreed to translate *The Silent Road* and add an Introduction. What she has done is to produce a parody of the book and I shudder to think what serious reviewers will say about its contents. Some of what she writes shows her perception, but most of it seems to be set down in intense nervous haste. Am I unfair? Well, you can judge when you read the book for yourself. I am lauded to the heavens and constantly referred to as 'Major Pole'. We can only hope that this travesty will soon pass into its deserved oblivion. And to have to autograph copies of it!

Later. I may have been too critical of S.S.C. and I am sure she has slaved to do her best most unselfishly.

It is only that eulogy focussed on me causes both rage and sadness. Sadness because, having missed so many opportunities of service, I feel that my life has been a failure.

29.3.63

Well my Dear, how pleased I was to glimpse you and your delightful companion at Glastonbury. But how awfully boring for you to be sitting almost in my lap during WTP's talk at Little St. Michael's! A front seat in the stalls at any performance is entirely without charm.

I wonder whether our dates stand for Paris? 18/22 April. Don't let this project oust from your mind the more intimate undertaking associated with our Chalice Well courtyard. At this spot over the centuries, many thousands of healings have happened; and many more (D.V.) should follow.

* Simone Saint Clair. Writer and translator. Heroine of *The French Resistance* and author of *Ravensbrück l'Enfer des Femmes*. Died 1975.

My prayer is that you shall both enjoy a peaceful and an inspiring Eastertide. And that the weather will be kind.

I too hate genuflexions, although I often bow low to the pure spirit of a tree or a spring of water.

Nearly all the manifold healings via the Chalice spring took place in that stone paved courtyard, which must be beautified and brought back into full use for that purpose. Also we must introduce music at Little St. Michael's, and I shall try to secure a good faithful record player. Which is the best, and which music do you feel has the most healing qualities?

Molten red hot lava is at present flowing down Etna's N.E. slopes towards a pine forest. Is this a challenge to action or a signal for delay?

I wish our T.V. affair could be recorded; so that any awful malaprops could be corrected before the programme goes out. I take part in all sorts of dramas, plays and discussions put on for the benefit of denizens in Borderland, without any nerves. But I hate taking part in such affairs on earth. Why the difference?

Another appeal has come in for WTP to undertake an American and Canadian 'lecture tour', talking all day and travelling all night . . . and for seven days every week. Will you please go instead? (Not much to ask, is it?)

15.4.63

Unless the heavens fall I shall arrive in a taxi at or just before 1 p.m. on Thursday and will keep the taxi.

Your hints about music both for the film and for Little St. Michael house are going to prove *more* than valuable.

The last Abbot of Glastonbury (Whiting) was hung, drawn and quartered, mainly because he would not tell Henry's Commissioners where the immensely valuable Abbey plate, silver and jewels had been hidden. (Never found since and believed to be somewhere beneath Chalice Hill, which was then Abbey property.)

Have spent a quiet but fully occupied Easter, much missing the use of the lovely home which took me fifty years to build and equip.

Hotel Cecilia,
Paris
20.4.63
8 a.m.

Let us give thanks

In the times that are to be, the full reasons for our thanksgiving now will become clearly evident. Let us give thanks. There is joy in the heart of one who is closer to you than the very breath of life. And whose loving presence has been your companion throughout your present pilgrimage and can never desert you nor leave you desolate and alone.

It is for you to know that it is a very dear wish of hers that what follows should receive an echo of willing acceptance in your mind and heart and thought and whole being.

The seeds now being sown, yes even during these few days in Paris, are destined to bear fruit beyond, far beyond our present understanding. The true Message of the Grail is once more to shine forth with power and inspiration, bringing with it a revealing illumination to the hearts and minds of men.

Half a century ago, in the Women's Quarter at Glastonbury, from the depths of the Well of St. Bride, a Cup was brought out into the light of day. This vessel is the symbol of the heavenly and eternal Grail, the Chalice of the Christ, the Promise of the future. Within a year of its recovery and *on that very spot*, the Celtic seer Fiona MacLeod wrote the following words:

> From the silence of time
> Time's silence borrow.
> In the heart of today
> Lies the WORD of tomorrow:
> The builders of JOY
> Are the Children of Sorrow.

The sorrow referred to is not the self-pity with which we have mistakenly clothed this wonderful word. It is the sorrow from which through Divine Alchemy the Christ lifted Jesus into the glory of His Ascension: an Ascension that heralds with certitude upliftment for us all, and for all manifestations of Life throughout the seven kingdoms of nature. Let us distil from our own sorrows the joy and the promise of our own upliftment through our dedication to selfless service.

28.4.63

Well well here we are more or less in shreds and tatters. *You* however with the spirited resilience of youth can take such hectic goings-on in your stride.

The highlight for you of course, was renewal of contact with G.M.* and your interior recollection of your intimate and joyful relationship with him in early Renaissance France. For me, of course, the highlight was the unexpected summons to attend a Conference of Arthur and his Knights. He has become an Initiate and in some ways an Elder Brother, available for the service of those who are developing 'second sight'. Being one of the great Orders working under the banner of Michael it is natural that Arthur and his Cavaliers should be concerned once more with human affairs, now at this supreme turning point and time of crisis. Perhaps therefore the door that opened during our Paris sojourn, and using G.M. in some way? has allowed Arthurian vibrations to enter the mind and soul of France in some special manner? 'A seed is sown.' I am only guessing. Anyway *we were used*, and for important purposes, despite all the external frip-frap.

Can you draw some parallel between the Two Tables, both sanctified by a Cup and by the spiritual significance of the Grail/Chalice as the supreme symbol of brotherly love on a universal scale: Jesus' table of the last of the seven suppers, and Arthur's Round Table of Chivalry?

(No, alas! – I couldn't! R.L.)

* Gabriel Marcel.

23

I wonder whether you are now consigning my scribbles to the fire? It is true that, Providence and yourself being willing, I hope that you will feel able to interpret WTP and what he tries to stand for, when he has gone on elsewhere. Few know anything about me or why I am 'down here' just now. Nevertheless much of what I write to you about is only of passing interest and not worth retaining.

My job in your case is to help you to open your own inner doors of perception. This task would only be hindered were I to interpret your own past for you, rather than allowing it to unfold naturally. Mediums sometimes stand in the way of true development. For instance let the memories of your past contacts with G.M. in France and Lombardy come back to you *naturally*.

We are all far too inclined to look backwards, and even to revere the past. For me it matters not whether the whole Arthurian saga consists mainly of myth, so long as these myths can still prove useful in pointing *forward* to a greater spiritual fulfilment for the race.

I have been told that of Joseph of Arimathea's twelve disciples (who sat round a well rather than a table), one defaulted badly. And the same regarding one of Arthur's Twelve. Very curious if so, following the same sequence after Jesus' last and seventh supper. (By the way, who WTP was then is of no importance.)

Ask Sally to impress you during sleep, because you can't remain dependent for conscious contact on intermediaries forever.

(I still chuckle at the way your face fell when your soothsayer predicted that the man you were to meet would be elderly! So unromantic, such a let-down and so contrary to all your youthful aspirations.)

Well Alexias my dear we do seem to have set several chariots rolling along their destined way. Perhaps one of them after completing its present missionary journey will return to carry me aloft (or below) and leave the field free for others to plough, sow and reap. So far as TP is concerned he would much prefer any harvest of his sowing to be reaped without reference to the sower. However, a Source whose authority I dare not gainsay places this wish beyond my reach.

Of the 1940–44 period it might be mentioned that apart from war work and civil defence duties, TP toured the country speaking in churches, halls, and to troops in training, especially in connexion with the Silent Minute and its significance. (*Inter alia* of course he brought up, educated, and sent his three children out into the world.)

I received a second summons to Arthur's celestial Court. This time I was allowed to journey there on my own beloved steed (with a squire and page also mounted, quite a cavalcade). Among much else I am expected to render the Chalice Well paved courtyard fitting once more to act as an exterior anchorage and focal point for 'Round Table' conferences, for Arthur's own use.

7.5.63

Yes Hester Dowden was remarkable for her sincerity and single-mindedness. I think Johannes was a real person and, as is inferred, closely related at one time to the Plotinus influence.

Everyone I have ever talked to who knew Jesus on earth describes him differently. Not at all surprising. When angry or indignant, Jesus appeared to grow in stature, his features and eyes darkened and his whole personality seemed to change. Then again when allowing Christ to speak through him, Jesus' body seemed to become luminous, his hair and eyes lightened and he looked magnificent. I remember him as of medium height, blue-grey eyes (that could darken and sparkle suddenly); sun-tanned, auburn beard and hair. He was very well built, most lithe and agile, with the springy step of a man in perfect health. His very litheness seemed at times to increase his height and 'presence'. He was fond of sleeping outdoors under the stars and sky, quite unperturbed by wind or rain or cold. He liked to get up very early when all the others slept on, and go for long walks across the hills and up and down the valleys; covering immense distances in incredibly short time. And turning up for the morning meal at the point of his departure, as fresh as ever.

I was no one in particular, but there was an occasion when I was allowed to walk with him on one of these early morning excursions. It took us along the upper reaches of the Jordan, N.E. of the Lake and in the direction of snow-capped Mount Hermon. Though young and hardy I could only keep pace with breathless difficulty, and for most of the time there was a lovely silence, filled with peace and an inner restfulness. It was later on this very occasion that I learned much of what I am allowed, at long last, to share with others: the true meaning of life, and time and eternity; the resistless power of selfless love; what compassion really means, the significance of the stillness of great silence; the oneness of life in every Kingdom and throughout the infinite majesty of all the Universes. Ah me! How little I took in or fully understood at the time. And how long it has taken even to try to fulfil what was laid upon me then. I am indeed filled with shame.

Let the young man who fled naked*, preserve his anonymity, for he is alive today and to my knowledge doing good work. The linen cloth he left behind him was destined to serve a great purpose. Yes, he feared much, but he was no traitor.

But why ask *me* questions? You have all the Records, you can browse among those Akashic accounts of Jesus' earthly life and the surrounding circumstances. Every time I think I have met your wishes, you ask *more* questions and I have to begin all over again. . . . (This is *not* a complaint!)

---

* TP is replying to a question of mine about this mysterious young man of St. Mark's Gospel.

Well Alexias, are you really resting?

Am interested in S.S.C's article in the current *Light*. Your translation?* Murmurs reach me about 'La R. du G.' and its 'author', but I have now passed on to other matters and we will let the bus run . . .

I sent you a line from home yesterday. No doubt I am indiscreet, but what I tell you privately about Jesus won't see the light of day during my lifetime. He never got on very well with his father. Jesus was such an out of doors boy that he could not stand working at his father's carpentry and was much closer to his uncle, Joseph of Arimathea: and spent a great deal of time with him, and on his boats and in J. of A's lovely hill house and gardens in Judaea. The stories about his visits to India and Tibet during his early twenties are apocryphal. He *did* travel widely, during sleep; in the way TP does, when he goes to the Kremlin, Washington and elsewhere (but of course, far more expertly than TP). He may have appeared in many places in the Orient and elsewhere in this way.

Jesus did go on several sea trips with his uncle, when in his teens, and thoroughly enjoyed himself away from home restrictions. Above an ancient archway in the Chapel of Plas (Roseland in Cornwall) there is a very early inscription recording his sojourn there with J. of A. on their way to Glastonbury. This may well record no more than a tradition, but it is a persistent one. Jesus was a constant source of anxiety to his mother, because he would disappear for days on end during his teens; and then turn up without adequate, or any, explanation! The early morning walk I referred to took place when Jesus was twenty-three, and *before* the mantle of Christ had fully clothed him. He was of course an Initiate in his own right, but he did not fully comprehend the significance of the coming stupendous overshadowing, during his youth, or even when he met John the Baptist for the first time.

The accretions of later years and centuries about his early life and pre-baptismal days should be taken with a grain of salt. In those early days there was no discussion about any immaculate conception. I am sure his followers and his own family never

---

* Yes.

believed this. There is a document in existence, inscribed on mica plates, written by Polycarp when he was acting as John's secretary on Patmos. This contains John's own memoirs, dictated from memory when he was an old man, and there are no references there to virgin births and the rest.

I know where this unique mica scroll lies buried; but apparently the time is not ripe for its recovery and publication. (Jesus' father had two sons by a concubine, both younger than Jesus, but they died early, to their father's lasting sorrow.) I doubt whether these and many similar facts will ever be revealed to the world. But they are clearly inscribed upon the Akashic Records; and so in due course you will be able to examine them at your leisure.

10.5.63

Returning once more to the times of Jesus, much in my mind at present: he usually spoke Aramaic, the colloquial tongue of the period. Aramaic contains no Imperative. 'Thou shalt not' would have to be worded differently, for instance 'it is not seemly' to do this or that. Therefore it was only when Jesus' sayings were translated into Greek (and then Latin) that the denunciatory tone crept in. When beings calling themselves 'Teachers' communicate from the Invisible and use imperative or denunciatory language, one knows at once that they are bogus.

Did you know why the mustard seed was used in relation to faith? Commonly supposed, I believe, on account of its small size. But there are many other seeds smaller still. So I went to enquire and this is what I was 'told':

'The mustard seed is the only known seed which is pure, in that it cannot be hybridized or grafted with a seed or plant of any other species.' I wonder if this is confirmed botanically?

I have often wondered how Jesus' career would have been affected had there been friendly relations between him and Joseph

his father. The latter had the craftsman's resentment of mendi-
cancy and the sort of gypsy life led by his son for so long. Had it
not been for his uncle's generosity, Jesus and those who gave up
their living to follow him would often have been in sore straits.
The stories of bread and fishes galore were parables devised later,
and the events on which they were based were by no means of the
miraculous magnitude that we are led to believe. The lot of
wanderers dependent on the alms of the friendly is a hard one
indeed.

Like all great Initiates, before or since, Jesus never performed
'miracles' unless in dire extremity or for healing purposes. Once
when laid up by a severe attack of malaria he refused to heal
himself by performing an instantaneous cure. Nor would he use his
clairvoyant faculty to sidetrack personal obstacles or daily
hindrances. Sad that later writers should have glossed and
exaggerated so much in order to underline his 'Divinity'. I never
heard him use an imperative even when speaking in Greek. But his
merest *suggestion* carried a power, authority and certitude, which
could not be gainsaid.

12.5.63

Notes

An exoteric and summarized version of the Akashic Records
exists; and is sometimes tapped, often by 'chance', by truth
seekers. The vibrations left on our planetary ether by the life and
acts of Jesus are still strong, and can appear in the form of a
cinema serial. People who happen to tap such a Record often
begin to identify themselves with this or that character around
Jesus. If egocentric they end by seeing themselves as actual
participants; and as a result people alive today say they were
Peter or John or Mary etc., irrespective of the fact that there are
many other such claimants. This does not rule out the truth that

many alive in Jesus' time are now in incarnation again, as our New Age reaches its dawn. You will never meet an Initiate or an Adept who will reveal his or her past identities, it is against the Rules to do so.

The Gospel narratives that have come down to us are not eyewitness accounts of the events narrated. They are hearsay, sometimes based on the memory of illiterate men and women: however, a mystery is involved here, namely that on occasion the writers of the Gospels, and some other N.T. recorders, wrote clairvoyantly and clairaudiently, in order that a modicum of truth might be passed down to future generations.

As an instance, Jesus being an Initiate would never have breathed to a soul details of his temptations, communion with Satan and so on (of which there were no observers). The record of these events has come down to us in the way described above.

Being human, we long for first hand accounts. 'I was little more than a boy when Jesus stayed a night or two with my parents, I being their only son. At that time we lived on a farmstead near Tyre, and I spent most of my time working in our fields, and occasionally fishing. I still remember how Jesus looked and spoke, and how he gave us all great joy, this being long before he became famous and swallowed up among the multitudes.

'Toward sunset on the first day of his stay with us, he came out of the guest room where he had been praying and told me to fetch a stool. We walked up to the village well where he sat down, then asked me to gather the children of our neighbours. As we sat around him he began to ask us questions about the everyday things that filled our lives. Then he told us such wonderful stories about the birds and the trees and the flowers; how to speak to them and live with them; how when he went swimming in Galilee and Jordan he would speak to the fishes and live their lives with them.

'Later, my mother and many of her friends came to the well to fill their pitchers. Jesus helped them draw up the water from the well, and when each pitcher was filled, he blessed it and the water in it.

'Mother sent me to fetch father from the inn, telling him to come home quickly so that he could share with us the water that Jesus had blessed. I shall remember those two happy days forever and forever.'

If only we had narratives like that instead of the history of events set down long after they occurred! By the way, it is based on fact.

Jesus was probably about thirty when baptized by John. How wonderfully had he retained his near-anonymity since the age of twelve! No wonder his own family were often puzzled and estranged! To them, some of his remarks suggested that he felt no particular ties with them. Indeed so loose were those ties that on occasion Jesus as a boy would not be missed from the household until he had been absent for several days! If only his uncle Joseph (said by some erroneously to have been his *great*-uncle) had left a diary of the way he looked after the youth and early manhood of his nephew! Of his love of the sea, of boating and swimming. Of how he never fished for food or to kill, was often in communion with sea and river creatures and the very spirit of the Waters. How he helped his uncle and his cousin Josephes on their farm, milking the cows, tending the sheep, helping the arrival of calves and lambs. Climbing the olive trees to beat down the olives. Laughing and shouting.

17.5.63

I was so sleepy when I scribbled my last notes to you that I cannot remember whether they included the sequel to your young man's precipitate flight. The Captain of the High Priest's guard sent one of his men after the youth, with instructions to bring him back at all costs; he regarded the incident with suspicion, as possibly part of a plot to rescue Jesus.

Now nothing happens by accident, and the details of all cosmic events are prepared, centuries before such events take place outwardly. The soldier, known by the name Kopul (spelling no doubt incorrect), carrying with him the youth's garment, chased him up the slopes of Mount Scopus and down into the wooded valley that slopes towards the Dead Sea. The chase was unsuccessful, and when Kopul returned to the garden it was empty, Jesus

31

having been taken away in close custody. And everyone else had disappeared.

In the days when Mary Magdalen was generous with her favours, Kopul had known her well. He always remained her friend, admiring her pluck and ready wit. In those days linen garments were valuable and a few days later K. felt impressed to hand over your young man's robe to Mary. It was in this way that when the latter was asked by J. of A. to help him prepare the grave clothes, this garment came into use (charged as it was with strong magnetic power). The terrible mutilations suffered by Jesus' body naturally affected the rhythm of his etheric counterpart: and it was for this reason that this particular garment was used.

N.B. Now the above record is *not* altogether first hand and so I cannot vouch for its accuracy in every detail. However, as evidently some link exists between you and the youth in question, you may one day be able to verify the circumstances for yourself. I don't suppose that the data you are collecting on these subjects is to remain indefinitely hidden under a bushel. In the Latter Days all will be uncovered. Meanwhile it is at your own discretion with whom you share it, and there is no reason why you and they should not regard the disclosures as apocryphal, if that is how they strike you. The training of the imagination to reject falsehood and illusion is a task as difficult as it is vitally important.

17.5.63

It is laid upon me to answer your questions to the best of my poor ability; this I try to do and you should ignore any seeming grumbling.

The Cup. Yes I will post you fully in due course. Astralitis has invaded the whole episode and causes even me annoyance at times. NO CLAIMS whatever are made by TP on this Cup's behalf.

The Seven Suppers. Naturally Jesus was constantly taking meals with his close followers, and often with friendly hangers-on. But he gave *esoteric* teaching to selected disciples at what are occultly known as the 'Six Suppers', which preceded at intervals the 'Last Supper'. Someday this hidden teaching will be revealed.

One cause of confusion is the fact that *three* of his intimates bore the name of John (apart from John the Baptist). I may go into this another time. I shall never forget with what vigour and respectful solicitation the 'good man' tried to persuade Jesus to remain in his house for the night. He was horrified at the plan to go out into the darkness, especially when revolution was in the air, with the intention of spending the night out of doors. He offered his donkey for Jesus to ride, and the services of his own close kinsman as a protection. But it seemed as if Jesus was in a trance; he answered not but led the twelve out into the garden and on to the hill slopes beyond. (I have often tarried there in my present incarnation, both physically and otherwise.)

Your young man was virile and possessed a particular kind of magnetism with which the linen robe he wore had become impregnated. No accident that it formed a major portion of the grave clothes! It was needed to preserve the etheric double whilst Jesus was in the tomb. Your young man when he touched Jesus in the garden had a sudden vision of the horrors of the approaching tragedy, more than he could stand. And so he fled, not even knowing of the service he had been destined to render.

When Jesus first appeared to Mary M. and said 'Touch me not', it was because his etheric counterpart was not yet fully material-ized. Later however when he was fully materialized it is recorded that he appeared to two disciples in *'another form'*. I think it is Mark who records this significant statement.

I have never seen a reasonable explanation from theologians of the lament upon the Cross. Quite out of character. But one must remember that the Christ, the Cosmic Being who overshadowed Jesus for over three years, could not be crucified, nor could this cosmic overshadowing persist during the Crucifixion. It was not the Christ but Jesus the man who suffered 'death'. The lament was evoked when Jesus felt the Christ mantle being withdrawn – had the Christ remained within Jesus, then under no circumstances could 'death' have taken place. A mystery not easy of general comprehension. (Certainly Jesus himself did not fully understand what was going on at that time.)

Now *don't* accept anything I share with you simply on my authority. I beseech you to sift, sift, sift, always retaining your independence of judgement.

See how foolish TP can be! For many years he was troubled by the thought of J. of Arimathea's desertion of Jesus at a time when he most needed support: yet I only had to enquire in the right quarter to learn two salient facts – (1) that J. of A. was fighting for a reprieve up to the last; and was then forcibly held in Pilate's house for fear that his presence at the Cross would unleash a revolution. (2) That Jesus was destined to be 'alone' at that time; save for the three Marys and their escort.

Someday perhaps I will tell you about the truly cosmic significance of the Triad of Marys.

20.5.63

'The Cup of Peace', referred to often as the Cup of Avalon or Jesus Cup, came to light at St. Bride's Well (or Source) near the Brue Stream Glastonbury in October 1906. Not far from Cradle Bridge. Every effort to trace its origin and history has failed, in spite of half a century's intensive research throughout Europe, Palestine and the Near East. Nor has it been possible to check the accuracy of the story told by Dr. Goodchild in this connexion.*
Psychometric readings indicate that the object possesses an aura of antiquity and an atmosphere of sanctity: on the other hand many glass experts consider that this vessel is of modern origin, due to its fresh appearance and lack of antique patina.

However, one very knowledgeable glassmaker has stated: 'Due to the imperfections apparent in its manufacture, no modern craftsman would have allowed this specimen to be retained. Evidently the maker was working with inadequate tools, probably

* See following pages for WTP's summary of the finding of the Cup.

34

in sand in the open air, and signs of haste in the making are apparent.' (Objects subject to de-materialization and reappearance lose their qualities of age, renewing their youth when re-materialization takes place.)

Clairvoyant expertise seems to confirm both age and great sanctity.

A short account of the finding of the Cup at Glastonbury in 1906

It was in the Spring of 1902 that Wellesley Tudor Pole became first interested in Glastonbury and about that time had a dream in which he saw himself as a monk of the old Abbey. He subsequently visited Glastonbury on many occasions and in 1904 received the impression that some important find connected with the Christian Faith would come to light there. He also felt that he must find three maidens who would be willing to go to Glastonbury as pilgrims and fit themselves for possible work there and at other Celtic Christian centres. He later took his sister Katharine down to Glastonbury on pilgrimage and in the following year met Janet and Christine Allen whom he instinctively felt would be suitable for spiritual activities connected with the birthplace of Christianity in England.

In November 1905 Janet and Christine Allen made their first pilgrimage to Glastonbury. Early in 1906 WTP visited Glastonbury once more, strong in the faith that a precious and holy object was hidden there which should if possible be brought to light. In August 1906 whilst sitting in his Bristol office he had a clear vision of a particular spot, a well, overshadowed by a thorn tree on the route taken by pilgrims and reverenced by them, owing to the traditional belief that the ground there had been hallowed by St. Bride and her followers. At this spot WTP 'saw' a buried object that appeared to give a radiant light.*

* This well and the thorn tree above it have now disappeared as the result of irrigation operations. A stone slab marks the spot.

During September neither he nor his sister was able to visit Glastonbury, but Janet and Christine Allen were on the point of going on pilgrimage; so that without mentioning his vision WTP suggested that they might clear out the well and report on anything of interest they found there. This they did on September 3rd and on returning to Bristol reported the finding of many small trinkets apparently left by earlier pilgrims, and also a glass saucer or Cup of considerable beauty. When found it was entirely caked with mud. They were deeply impressed by this vessel; and after washing it in the Brue stream replaced it in the well where they had found it.

WTP did not at first connect the finding of this glass Cup directly with his earlier vision, but a day or two later he received a letter from a Dr. J. A. Goodchild then living in retirement at Bath, containing an enclosure which he requested should be handed to the pilgrims who had just visited Glastonbury. This letter contained the drawing of a 'Cup Sign' that Dr. Goodchild stated he had seen in the sky on the afternoon of September 3rd 1906 and which he felt was in some way connected with Glastonbury. Thinking that this sign might indeed be connected with the vessel found in the well, Janet and Christine Allen visited Dr. Goodchild and told him of their find. On hearing their story and the description of the vessel Dr. Goodchild appeared to be greatly moved, and told them that he had reasons for believing that the Cup was a holy relic, once actually used and carried by the Master Jesus. He gave no reasons for this statement nor did he make any further comments at that time.

Dr. Goodchild's Story

On hearing the result of Janet and Christine Allen's visit to Dr. Goodchild, WTP, who had met him on previous occasions, went to Bath with his sister Katharine and was told the following story.

36

Early in 1885 Dr. Goodchild when staying at Bordighera in Italy was told by a friend that two remarkable pieces of glass, a platter and a saucer-shaped Cup, were to be seen in a local tailor's shop. He went to see them, and was told by the tailor that they had recently been found in a small stone receptacle in the wall of an ancient Monastery surrounding his father's vineyard at Albegna. Dr. Goodchild bought both vessels from the tailor for £6 and brought them back to England and showed them to his father. His father appeared to be very interested. He asked his son whether he realized what he had found – took possession of both vessels, but suggested that the Cup should be shown to Sir A. Franks of the British Museum in order to obtain some idea as to its possible age and value. This was done, and Sir A. Franks gave it as his opinion that this vessel was of ancient workmanship and design: certainly not of modern manufacture. Dr. Goodchild senior then locked away both vessels and they remained with him until his death. When in Paris in 1898, Dr. Goodchild junior stated that he had a strange experience in which while partly awake he heard a voice telling him that the Cup in his father's keeping was one that had been carried by Jesus and was destined to have a powerful influence in the shaping of thought in the coming century. He was further instructed that as soon as possible after his father's death he should take the Cup to Bride's Hill in Glastonbury and deposit it there according to instructions to be given later. Some short time later his father died; and acting on instructions his son sent the platter to a member of the Garibaldi family in Italy; and the Cup he brought to England later the same year. Dr. Goodchild then looked up an old map of Glastonbury and found on it a place called Bride's Hill or Beckery. Three weeks later when staying at Bath and on Monday, September 3rd 1898, he was awakened out of sleep by a voice telling him to take the Cup to a well on Beckery at Glastonbury and leave it there. This he did; and between the years of 1898 and 1906 he visited Beckery annually. In 1900 he looked to see if he could find any trace of the vessel; but the well had been cleaned out and the Cup was apparently no longer there.

Although WTP had met Dr. Goodchild on several occasions at Bath and Bristol between 1902 and 1906 and had discussed Christian origins connected with Glastonbury, the subject of the existence of the Cup had never been mentioned. Dr. Goodchild definitely stated that the only person he had mentioned it to was William Sharp (Fiona Macleod) whom he had told during a visit to Glastonbury on August 1st 1904. After hearing this story from Dr. Goodchild K.T.P. went to Glastonbury at WTP's wish on the 1st October 1906 and found the Cup where it had been left by Janet and Christine Allen as already related. She brought it back to Clifton where it was placed in a shrine in WTP's home at 16 Royal York Crescent, Clifton.

Whilst none of those concerned had any adequate reason to doubt Dr. Goodchild's veracity, it should be stated that no objective evidence of the truth of his story has ever been discovered.

WTP and his friend Mr. Frederick Leveaux visited Bordighera on two occasions in the 1930's but could find no trace of Monastery ruins at Albegna nor could local inhabitants throw any light on the incidents related by Dr. Goodchild above. The sole authority for his statements rests therefore on his own account of the events stated by him to have occurred.

Authorities consulted on the possible age of the Cup

In December 1906 WTP showed the Cup to the Very Rev. Dom Gasquet (Abbot President of the English Benedictines), who expressed the opinion that it was of ancient manufacture, possibly of the Imperial Roman or Graeco-Roman era.

Mr. Reed of the British Museum gave his opinion that it was a clever copy of Imperial Roman work.

On December 15th 1906 Dom Gasquet, who later became a Cardinal obtained the expert opinion of his brother and of certain

Birmingham authorities including Chance Brothers and they were unanimous in their belief that the Cup was of ancient manufacture mainly owing to the signs of wear of both water and earth on the base and outer rim of the vessel.

On December 22nd 1906, the Very Rev. Mgr. Barnes of Cambridge gave it as his opinion that the vessel dated from between the beginning of the Christian era and A.D. 500.

On January 26th 1907 Mr. Wilde of the South Kensington Museum expressed several diverse opinions as to its possible date.

1. Probably Phoenician or Roman of about 500 B.C.
2. Manufactured in Venice in the Middle Ages.
3. Finally he felt that the wonderful preservation of the Cup pointed to its not being ancient but of some date in the last century. He based this last view on the fact that the glaze was so perfectly preserved.

On June 22nd 1907 WTP took the Cup to London to be examined by Sir William Crookes and Archdeacon Wilberforce. Sir William was of the opinion that it was of great age and requested that it might remain in his care in order to make a more minute examination. Finally he felt that it was very old, the Maltese pattern between the glass being a pre-Christian sign. His account of the probable method of manufacture is attached to these notes.

Archdeacon Wilberforce was anxious that a meeting of experts should be held and also of people likely to be interested. This meeting was held on July 20th 1907 at 20 Deans Yard, Westminster, when WTP gave those present the story of the finding of the Cup at Glastonbury in 1906.

On January 27th 1908 a second meeting was held at Archdeacon Wilberforce's house at which three archaeological experts, Dr. Ginsberg, Mr C. H. Read and Mr. J. Cobb, were present. After a careful examination of the Cup had been made, the general opinion was expressed that owing to its wonderful preservation it could not be of really ancient origin and was probably therefore of fairly modern manufacture.

On March 25th 1913 Gisela M. A. Richter of the Metropolitan Museum of Art in New York wrote: 'With regard to the photograph of your bowl it looks like typical millefiori. These bowls date from the first century A.D. To judge from the photograph your specimen appears to be ancient, not a Venetian imitation, but it is impossible to pass final judgement without seeing the original.'

Between 1908 and 1950 the Cup was shown to a number of other archaeological students and experts, the majority of whom took the view that this vessel *was* of ancient make, and may well have been manufactured at Antioch in the first century A.D.

Efforts to trace the Cup's history

During July and August 1907 certain information was received by WTP from various esoteric sources relating to evidence of the proof of the identity of the Cup in the form of ancient scripts which it was stated could be found at a certain spot in Constantinople. On August 20th 1907 WTP left England to visit Constantinople in an endeavour to identify the spot which had been described as situated between the Mosque of St. Sophia and the sea coast. He was able to identify what he felt to be this spot, but owing to the proximity of the Harem Gardens and to the fact that it was within the precincts of the Seraglio the place was closely guarded and close access was quite impossible.

In December 1907 WTP again visited Constantinople and as a result of further research he formed the opinion that the scripts he was searching for were no longer concealed at the spot in question. On several occasions during the 1930's and 1940's WTP carried out archaeological research work in old Istanbul, mainly beneath the ruins of the House of Justinian on the Sea Walls. He was helped in this work by Sir David Russell and Mr. Frederick Leveaux, and extensive excavations were made in the effort to locate the underground rock chambers said to have once housed the famous Library of Justinian the Great. Due to the outbreak of war in 1939, this work was given up before tangible results had been achieved. Work in the same area was renewed on several occasions between

1945 and 1952, but without reaching the objective in question. Due to political difficulties and financial problems no further work has been carried out at this site up to the present time (1958).

Origin of the Cup

It is evident that the actual origin and history of the Cup are likely to remain a mystery. Apart from a number of clairvoyant and psychometric investigations (the results of which have proved conflicting) no objective evidence of any kind has so far come to light in regard to this vessel's identity or age. The concensus of opinion based on esoteric research tends to indicate that this Cup is not modern and may quite possibly date from Antioch in the first century of the Christian era.

Its finders, in the total absence of authentic data, do not claim any especial sanctity for the Cup, in relation for instance to the idea that it may have some association with the Grail traditions. It should be stated, however, that many people have experienced remarkable visions when in the presence of this Cup, some of which appear to be directly linked with incidents connected with the Last Supper. Others have attested to the fact that this vessel appears to radiate an aura of peace and healing. It has come to be called 'The Cup of Peace'. In a symbolical sense the emergence of this Cup at the beginning of this century and from the 'Women's Quarters' of Glastonbury is an event of considerable significance. The Piscean Age, symbolized by the Cross and the Fish, is drawing to its close. We are now entering the Aquarian Age symbolized by the Cup (or pitcher) and the Man. (Or as Jesus put it, by the 'Sign of the Son of Man', as set forth in his prophecy concerning the Second Coming in *St. Matthew* Ch. 24, *St. Luke* Ch. 21 and *St. Mark* Ch. 13). The recovery of this Cup therefore at Glastonbury (the cradle of the Christian Faith in England) at this juncture in human history may have an important Message for the world. The emergence of the Cup of Peace in our times may well signify the promise through which the Cross of duality and suffering will be gradually transmuted into the Cup of unity and peace. It also

41

may have emerged as a herald of One who is to come as a Divine Messenger to Mankind for the new Age, and also as a 'Jesus sign' and to act as a reminder of the value of the Grail traditions of chivalry, purity and courage. . . .

The present custodians of the Cup intend to deposit this record of its finding with the vessel itself, for the guidance of posterity and in the hope that its mission to Mankind may be fulfilled in the times that are to come.

WTP

THE CUP
(Description by Sir William Crookes)

The Cup is a saucer-shaped vessel 136 millims outside diameter and 23 millims deep at the centre. It is about 7 millims thick, but varies slightly in places. The curvature is roughly spherical, i.e., a segment of a sphere 56 millims would fall within the thickness of the glass. It is formed of two surfaces, each from two to four millims thick and separated by fragments of silver leaf.

Each surface is built up of squares of glass mosaic having on them a beautiful design like a double Maltese cross. The obverse is made up of 25 to 30 of such squares arranged in 7 rows, 4, 5 and 6 pieces in the centre rows and a less number in the top and bottom rows; reverse not so many.

From the appearance of the ground work, it appears as if the mosaics originally were about 24 millims square and 4 millims thick, the great distortion of all but the centre ones being caused by subsequent fusion and moulding into shape. Each mosaic square has been sliced off a compound bar of glass made somewhat as follows:

A thick rod of green glass is taken as a centre, and round it are packed four triangular lumps of reddish-brown glass, with the blunt points inwards, so that the cross-section will be like a Maltese cross. Lozenge-shaped pieces of the same reddish-brown are then packed between the arms, so as to form in section a double Maltese cross. Thinner rods of green glass are now packed outside

42

each of the 8 points of the cross and the whole mass is heated in a furnace to the softening point and then dipped into a bath of clear colourless glass of a little lower fusing point. When well cemented together by the clear glass the whole lump is roughly fashioned to a rectangular shape and then drawn into a bar about 24 millims square. While still hot, but hard, it is cut into slices about 4 millims thick by sudden blows with a hatchet-shaped tool. It is seen that each slice will thus form a mosaic having on it an ornamental, double Maltese cross set in a square of clear glass. These square mosaics are then fitted together and at red (softening) heat squeezed into contact.

In the Cup the joints can be traced by streaks of air bubbles, showing that the main rod of composite glass had been allowed to cool and condense moisture, or has become soiled on the surface. This interferes with perfect union between two pieces of glass. An examination of the different mosaics where they have not been too much distorted by fusion, shows that they have been cut from the same compound rod, for it is possible to trace little peculiarities in the formation of the pattern through each piece.

For instance, taking the four small lozenge-shaped pieces between the four arms of the cross, it is seen that each has a definite character. One is more pointed at each end, another is pointed at one end and more round at the other, while another has a small flaw at the outer end. These peculiarities run through all the mosaics, and prove that they have all been cut from the same compound rod. From careful examination I think the workman made an oblong sheet of mosaic glass large enough to form the obverse and reverse of the Cup. When in a soft plastic state one half was laid on a convex mould of baked clay, silver leaf was then put between, and the rest of the half of mosaic turned over and squeezed down, the whole being returned to the furnace from time to time until all parts were melted together.

But on the reverse the soft glass naturally ran down to the sides, and it was forced or plastered back towards the centre, some of the mosaics hereby being distorted almost out of recognition. The obverse concave surface being supported by the clay mould would not suffer such distortion. When still soft an iron rod with a lump of glass on it, technically called 'punty', was stuck to the centre of the reverse side to act as temporary handle, and the vessel was trimmed at the edges with shears (these shear marks can now be seen). It was subjected quickly to a good heat to glaze the obverse surface and the cut edges and the temporary handle of glass removed by a drop of water and the vessel was cooled and annealed. The rough piece remaining is then ground off.

A careful scrutiny of the reverse side shows that the 'punty mark' has been ground off in the middle. The pattern does not go through, the mosaics on the obverse do not correspond in fashion with those on the reverse. The obverse side shows by certain circular markings on it that the mould in which it has been pressed had probably been turned on a potter's wheel, for circular markings on the mould are reproduced on the glazed surface. The reverse side must have originally been different thicknesses in different places, and after removing the 'punty mark', the whole has been roughly ground to bring it approximately to the same curvature as the obverse.

Another explanation of what I call the 'punty mark' may be suggested. The original vessel might have had an ornamental stem or foot. In Murray's Dictionary, under the heading 'Cup' it is said that 'the larger and more ornamental form (e.g., a wine cup or chalice) may have a stem or foot'. The stem might have been broken off by accident and the remaining fragment ground away, so as to preserve the upper portion as a shallow cup.

I have now described the mode in which I imagine the Cup may have been fashioned. The modes of glass working detailed are such as are in use in most large glass houses at the present day and do not differ materially from what we know were the methods of work in much earlier days. The workman who fashioned the Cup was an artist whose ideas were far in advance of the somewhat crude appliances at his disposal.

21.5.63

My reason for deluging you with scripts may have been obvious to Alexias. Zero hour for my Russian mission was approaching; and as I hardly expected to return, the idea was to provide you with all possible data beforehand. Now at the eleventh hour I hear that all the carefully worked out plans have been changed. I have no details yet, but for the time being what needs to be done behind the Iron Curtain, so far as WTP is concerned, will have to be carried out during sleep. Apparently priority is now being given to an urgent job here in the U.K. As I am thus to be given a respite (but not from Work!) the deluge should ease off!

Very rarely do angels materialize, but the Angels of the Passing, dedicated to serve Jesus, did so – among much else – in order *first* to remove the napkin from his head. By this means it was easier for his subtle bodies to emerge from his physical form and in time for him to be perceived by Mary M.

The Angels even took the trouble to fold this napkin and place it in a spot 'by itself' and specially 'wrapped together'. There is deep significance behind every incident of this kind.

The explanation given to me about the identity of the unknown disciple is so strange that, until I can verify it, the less said the better. This explanation does not really fit into the record that has come down to us, and opens up a vast new field of investigation and perhaps of illumination.

I can but surmise that you are being made the custodian of the intimations I have passed on to you, for a particular purpose. Perhaps in some way to be linked up with Avalon and the story of the Glastonbury Cup? And the Upper Room. Time will show you what is expected of you in these matters. Whenever something worth while falls into my lap, apart from giving thanks, I say to myself: 'This has come to you not because you deserve it, but because at this particular time and place it happened that no one really worthy could be found immediately available'. A sobering thought.

23.5.63

Dr. Goodchild was a clever but very eccentric medico, with a most lucrative practice at Bordighera for over thirty years. He was a bachelor, a Greek and Celtic scholar. His father was a well known

Victorian doctor, mystic and mathematician. It was only *after* the *Daily Express* got hold of the story of the Cup's finding that he came forward with his peculiar account of his connexion with this vessel. Of course the sceptic would regard the whole story as a concoction by TP and Goodchild in collusion: but what for? Gain? Notoriety? I have refused offers for this Cup in four figures and have spent many thousands over fifty-five years in trying to trace its external history. It is not for exploitation and I have nothing to gain from publicity. For me, this vessel provides a direct link with the time Jesus was on earth. In its presence it is almost certain that any question about his life or teaching would be answered correctly.

Psychometry has failed to prove the Cup's identity. For some undisclosed reason the vessel's true origin has been purposely concealed and still is. *Why?* I have it by me as I write this, and for the life of me I don't know how to shape its future destiny or whether to throw it into the sea.

Meanwhile I remain fuming with indignation over the Russian trip. Here have I been feverishly putting my house in order, only to be told the whole thing is off.

I hate the alternatives, human materializations and de-materializations are tricky substitutes for straightforward external undertakings. I am completely fed up!

Stephen the Seer. Stephen was a fine youth and a natural seer. He possessed the gift of prophecy, and with it the saintly quality of forgiveness. A very rare and lovely soul. Even after Saul had become his enemy and refused to save him from being stoned, Stephen told Saul (not recorded in Acts): 'We shall meet again, and as friends – not only in another world, but in this.' Adding the cryptic statement: 'When the very stone that slayeth me shall have seven eyes.' Meaning I suppose that the time will come when even the so-called lowest Kingdom, the mineral, shall be lifted up to possess vision of the unity of life, eternally present in all the seven Kingdoms of Nature: and presaging the Golden Age of universal brotherhood throughout *all* the Kingdoms. Does not Zechariah speak of a stone with seven eyes?*

* *Zechariah*, 3, 9–10.

Stephen. My information is *not* firsthand but hearsay, and so far I have been unable to trace the words he is said to have used to Saul, in the A. Records. (It involves such a long and difficult search.) Stephen was such a beautiful youth; Saul's enmity was roused by Stephen's rejection of his favours when Stephen was in his seventeenth year. Zechariah's writings, comparatively new at that time, were much under discussion and disputation in the temple and synagogues and this might possibly account for Stephen's mysterious allusion to a stone on which seven eyes were engraved. However, as I say, the words quoted cannot be vouched for by WTP.

I will try to answer your queries but do remember that I am *not* infallible. It takes me aback to discover repeatedly as I do that seers far above my status can at times seem to suffer from clouded vision.

Dematerialization etc.
The technique is bound up with a knowledge of rhythm, vibration, the sounding of key notes and their complementary 'answering' notes, as applied not only to matter including that of the human body but also to the etheric, astral and mental sheaths. Too complex to go into now.

Jesus was of medium height for a man, around five feet ten-and-a-half. The 'Church' pictures are wrong in making it appear that he was tall. Also his beard and hair were not black (like many Syrian

Jews) but medium brown with glints of gold – auburn. Eyes grey-blue, which became dark and flashing when his indignation was aroused. His beard was short, crisp and well kept and his hair did *not* go trailing all down his back. It was cleanly bunched around the nape of his neck, beautifully kept.

It is amazingly wrong that he should be depicted as rather effeminate and a mature but well-preserved sixty or so. He kept his youthful appearance right up to the end of his thirty-four years and was *not* a sight of terror and agony, even upon the Cross. During part of that ordeal he was in trance. At other times, when the pain was great he slipped out of his physical body and so was freed from agony – even lesser mortals can do this, as I know from experience; on a number of occasions, both in war and peace, I have done the same. But I do insist that his spirit and his high spirits kept him youthful and resilient throughout his life, despite the burdens he carried for those around him and for the whole human race. During his last three-and-a-half years the protective mantle of the Christ bore much of the burden for him, and lightened the sense of frustration and persecution.

6.6.63

More than delighted to hear that Alexias is rested and really refreshed! Don't come back to become submerged in a social whirl that will exhaust you anew. Lovely weather too on Iona, where the ceremonies proceed to plan. The Michael emblem is now installed in its permanent niche in the M. Chapel. All well.

My Whitsun has been somewhat tragic and very arduous. First an S.O.S. from my brother Alex in Mexico, gravely ill. Then there was a hitch in the reception arrangements for the Pope,* and I was very loth to be brought in. Releasing him from prolonged agony was slow and difficult. . . . Then the 'Left' are trying to arrange for his successor to be reactionary and the odds are about even. When

---

* Pope John's 'passing'.

I came home on Monday around 7.30 p.m. the house was filled with incense: from this I realized the Pope's release had come.

Then on Saturday late we were warned to prepare to receive about a hundred men, women and children, due to come over suddenly in an air crash. As a matter of fact, the crash off the Alaskan coast did not happen until late on Tuesday. Why our station was on the rota to deal with this particular tragedy, was not disclosed. However, enough of sad tidings.

Ireland in September sounds lovely. But long ago I gave up my freedom, and so have no idea what my instructions will be for that month or any other. Sometimes in my rebellious moments I feel like a kind of reluctant marionette; but then I pull up and go forward on my allotted way.

26.6.63

When enduring rather an ordeal (not of my making) a night or two ago, I suddenly glimpsed Jesus when he was about eighteen; standing in the sunlight poised for a dive into a deep pool in the river Jordan. He was out rambling with his cousin Josephes, when he saw a fox lying on the opposite bank of the river, with a damaged paw. To watch him dive in and swim over to the rescue, dazzled and inspired me and gave me back my joy.

On closer scrutiny I became convinced that it was not a fox, but a fine looking hare, of a breed larger than we see in England.

29.6.63

Before I comment on St. Francis etc., let me explain why I never quote textual authorities for the purpose of backing my outlook. (Steiner for instance, or Stainton Moses, or from the masses of modern mediumistic writings.) Directly I start reading books on these subjects, my own vision fades away and direct contacts (from *above* Astral levels) cease. On another plane, if I accept Nature's bounty at second hand via the flesh of animals, my mind and body and vision become confused. . . . Now all messages via mediums have perforce to come down *through* astral realms: these realms are fluid, a mere breath of etheric air at once disturbs this fluid condition and causes distortion and hence misinterpretation. If you look at yourself, for instance, in a clear pool of water the reflection can be quite accurate. But so soon as the water in the pool is disturbed, your reflection becomes disturbed also, and out of focus. Rarely nowadays is there any real serenity and stillness within these astral fluidic states.

I respect G. Cummins, but much of her automatic writing has been subject to the conditions I have tried to outline above. No true Initiate when he takes a body for temporary use labels himself with an antecedent name or personality. Therefore St. Francis was *not* a reincarnation of Jesus. There is however a mystery in this . . . Jesus having assumed for three years the mantle of the Christ experienced a permanent extension of auric potency – so much so, that segments of this potency can be *reflected* through humble and saintly beings like Francis or even Pope John XXIII.

Oh dear me how hard it is to explain clearly these arcane mysteries, without rousing ridicule or even abuse. But *you* will understand.

Jesus congenitally lame?* What absolute nonsense. It is true that when he was fifteen he barked his shin during a storm at sea in one of his uncle's ships en route from Jaffa to Alexandria (he was learning to handle the helm at the time). The resultant lameness lasted some weeks but never returned; although he *did* appear to be a little lame when carrying his Cross uphill, at the close of his earthly life.

St. Francis had a delicate physique and limped occasionally through weariness. Jesus was of noble athletic lithe build, more like a Greek athlete than a Jewish lad come of farming stock. Pictures showing him as gaunt and effeminate are pure nonsense. Come and see him with me, *for yourself*, on such an occasion as I

---

* I had read this in some psychic publication.

described to you the other day. Perfect symmetry, lovely alertness! Only Stephen of all the throng that followed later in his footsteps could begin to compare with Jesus in this respect. Banish from your vision the deplorable portraits that have come down to us from no contemporary artists.

31.6.63

Memo

In the current *Soleil* S.S.C. returns to her strange illusion that WTP's main purpose at Avalon is to unearth the veritable Holy Grail. Nothing in any of my writings or addresses lends any support to this assertion. The Grail has *never* materialized in mortal form to be handled by man. Nor ever will. This celestial symbol of Love and Unity has had its prototypes or earthly reflections from very ancient times. Of all spiritual symbols the Cup or Lotus is the most important and inspiring, far more so than the Cross, or Ankh, the Star or the Triangles: it epitomizes the heavenly Chalice, from which all mankind can freely drink together the wine of Divine inspiration and illumination. It is the one universal symbol that can unite in love and understanding men and women of every race, faith or creed, and it was with this meaning that Jesus used the (external) Cup at the last of his seven Suppers. Not until the Middle Ages did man begin to associate the Holy Grail of all the ages with the Cup used by Jesus.

If S.S.C. is referring to the Grail in this limited sense, then it is possible that Jesus' Cup may still be in physical existence. However it is not my object at Avalon to unearth it, even if by chance it is there. My aim is to prepare the Chalice Well property for use once more as a Gateway, through which the Christ's message for the New Age can enter and spread across the world. This very holy spot could in fact become once more the sounding board for a revelation of Divine Wisdom, attuned to the desperate needs of today's humanity.

I regard the discovery of the glass vessel from St. Bride's Well in 1906 as a promise or forerunner, symbolically, of Avalon's renewable destiny: 'a sign upon the wind'. No claim is made for its sanctity or age. No claim is made that this vessel (more like a saucer than a cup) was used at the Last Supper.* We do not know why its aura should seem to contain 'memories' of events associated with Jesus' life on earth. This mystery may never be solved, but in my view the soil of Avalon will not reveal any objects directly and *historically* linked with Jesus himself when in incarnation.

2.7.63

To chronicle in sequence psychometric glimpses or memories, would be to risk human imagining, an artificial effort to provide an historical record.

Glimpses can fade quickly and so seem to lose validity. One cannot force them into sequential order; but an editor of such scripts (jotted down as they are at the time of vision) could probably rearrange their order and so perhaps improve their lucidity. I think you now have the cream of these glimpses, and one cannot command sequels nor explanatory additions.

Viva voce questioning, in the presence of the Cup, *might* reveal further details or additional relevant information. But the recovery of Truth calls for spontaneity as an absolute pre-requisite. The responsibility of deciding how and with whom such experiences should be shared in these agonizing times, is a very real one. Some time a copy of all these intimations should be deposited with the Avalon Cup.

11.7.63

Yours dated today, arrived first post evidently before you had even written it. Is this your special brand of alchemy?

Some more 'findings' are now coming through about Jesus'

* See *The Awakening Letters*: The Glastonbury Scripts, Neville Spearman, 1978.

days; a kind of marginal commentary . . . ploughing with the oxen and the donkeys; and on more than one occasion riding away for many days, on caravan journeys, on the back of a camel. Retiring alone at certain seasons of the moon into caves and high places, and returning illumined and refreshed. Ditching and draining the fields and gathering wild herbs for the kitchen and for healing purposes. All this of course whilst he was still Jesus, the man, the hidden Initiate; and long before the last three years of his life when the mantle of the Christ descended upon him. In his aunt's kitchen he liked to help prepare and bake the unleavened bread, made into large 'scones' that could be broken by hand (never cut) and handed round at table. This bread with olives and figs and greenstuff were his favourite diet. Meat and fish he cared not for. And wine only on ceremonial occasions.

I suppose the greatest occasion in his life before Christhood was when he was twenty-five, having gone a journey into Syria and beyond with a party of Bedouins. Coming back alone and on foot he climbed Mount Hermon and there he was met and conversed with several of those great Beings who had achieved Christhood in the past. The Lord Buddha, Zoroaster, Confucius and some others unknown to our records. *What* a wonderful preparation this must have been for his own approaching Christhood!

Your own past lives. . . . All in good time. We must stick to priorities, realizing the urgency of the times we are living in. Look forward! Don't let your reading get in the way of your writing. That is, writing and thinking (for it) from within yourself and at first hand.

Enough for today!

On Thursday I go on my annual round of the Sussex curio shops. Wish me Luck.

2.8.63

Delightful to know you are near and in the sea during these sultry summer days. London is the limit just now and I am not going up again until Wednesday of next week.

May the renovation and beautifying of King Arthur's Courtyard at Chalice Well bring blessings to many, and not least to yourself! I will show you the Plan etc. before approval is given for the work to start. I am delighted! Why should we not make the best of both worlds by putting WTP on exhibition, say at a tenner a time, to recoup the outlay?

I was so pleased with your chatty and very human letter. Even if you *do* allow your serenity to be perturbed by this and that; and by the foolish vagaries of neurotic ladies. However I know you will retain your own poise and I praise the Gods that you possess plenty of commonsense. How *nice* therefore to be able to exchange thoughts and feelings without danger of misunderstanding, and on a level that is congenial both to you and to me! (Of course I cannot reach your mental heights but I can manage to pant along behind.)

Maybe the time has come to do a job together? Although *you* already have your plate as full as you care to see it?

I will return to this later in the epistle, and meanwhile will comment on yours.

Gurdjieff. Like so many occultists and especially those of Slavonic origin, he had no compunction in walking with the Gods and on other occasions consorting with the Devils. As a result he came into contact with many strange and powerful groups and movements, including the Energies of the Left Path who used Hitler as their external instrument. Has Denis Seurat written a book on G.; or are you relying on quotations in *Le Matin des Magiciens*?

Dr. Joel Carmichael's 'Death of Jesus', written by an erudite Jewish scholar, is a diabolically clever attempt to demote Jesus to the status of a political rebel; the leader of a kind of Mafia group who fully deserved his tragic end. Every scrap of available material is bent into use for this indictment, and most of the N.T. is 'shown' to be based on 'tendentious' and inaccurate records.

Probably this very skilful author suffers from a sense of racial guilt, but it will need an equally erudite biblical scholar to undo the harm this book has already done in America and will no doubt do over here. I think you will have to read it. I could send you my copy (and comments) a little later; and I wish that so much of cleansing value embedded in this astute and sinister volume could be lifted out.

I gather that I am now expected to allow my glimpses of Jesus' youth etc., to see the light of day. You have the originals, set down in haste and very clumsily. Shall we collaborate in preparing a small volume for publication?* Or would you prefer not? Could you be drawn into writing a Foreword?

Of course further spontaneous glimpses may follow, but I am apparently not expected to use this possibility as an excuse for delay. I should like to get Sir G. Trevelyan's comments before proceeding and also Raynor Johnson's, both of whom are friends and always willing to give me their views or advice. My fellow Chalice Well Trustees would expect me to dissociate them from any responsibility for the contents of such a publication. And at present I could not refer to the Avalon Cup as one of the major agencies for bridging two thousand years in time and space: a pity, this.

Well, put on your very attractive and many-pluméd thinking cap. And remember that you cannot hurt me by being frank, or critical or non-cooperative, as the case may be; in view of everything else that fills your plate just now.

13.8.63

I too am supposed to be redecorating my hovel but I don't quite know why. A mere man is at the mercy of any tradesmen he may call in, and don't they know it. Much hope all will go well with your Eaton Square renovations; but can't see why they are needed?

Am striving to mend a sixteen-year-old marriage, both partners being dear friends of mine. *Do* men and women, in the human bodily sense, really belong to the same species? If we incarnate in both kinds of body, more or less alternately, why in general is there so little true understanding between the sexes? How rare is a completely harmonious and satisfying marriage! How few couples know how to be *complementary* to one another.

Don't return that script. Pull it about. Set to work on a

* *A Man Seen Afar*, Neville Spearman.

55

commentary, perhaps sketch out a chapter? See what else should go in from other TP writings you have. Pray and meditate. Get into the atmosphere of the 1st century A.D., even if you look upon the Hebrews through Greek eyes.

Yes, of course I am still more or less a pagan. And so are you, especially in your guise as Alexias.

17.8.63

First about J.G.B.* – I am sure he could help you to understand better his and G's outlook and teaching. Far too complex for me and one can so easily become swamped in these intricate speculations. The occult path is complicated, devious, mesmeric. The eternal Truths are *simple*. Simplify! Let us take a page out of Jesus' uncomplex Book of Life.

So many earnest pilgrims, eagerly following the path of *knowledge*, find themselves lost in the byways.

22.8.63

Note

For an immeasurable period of time after the human form had emerged from purely animal structures, it contained a primitive soul which was entirely subject to animal instincts and sensations. The life essence even then belonged to the eternal order of being, but was not imbued with an individualized intelligence of its own. No historical or even legendary records remain to inform us of the first great Messenger to earth sent out through the Creative Hierarchy by Divine Command. His name and his mission are lost in the mists of time and he has long since passed beyond and above

* J. G. Bennett.

the confines of our solar system. It is allowed to be suggested that the main object of his coming was to bring with him the conditions through which the human soul could begin to incarnate in the bodily forms evolved for it but hitherto and still purely animal in function.

No doubt for evolutionary purposes still unrevealed to us, this descent brought about the duality which has led to the seemingly inevitable conflict in man between his animal and his human nature; a conflict which remains the dominating factor in the lives and experience of us all.

It was at that point in history, immensely distant from today, that the separation of the sexes took place. This sex division is hard for us to understand and would suggest that hitherto all forms of life on this planet had been sexless, yet capable in some way of self-proliferation.

Doubtless 'sex' as we know it, is only a comparatively temporary phase in the evolutionary process. According to the Greek, Jesus wrote upon the ground (the earth) on a certain famous occasion and not upon the sand. What he wrote has not yet been revealed, but I believe its significance was to become of permanent importance for the human race. At all times Jesus was deeply concerned with the problems of sex and the ceaseless conflict between man's higher and lower natures. Also with the double standard of morality, as prevalent in his times as it is in our own. In my view, by the action he took in this connexion, the assurance he gave to the woman taken in adultery would be rendered more permanent in its effects: the remarkable reference to the 'light of the world' which followed should not escape our notice in this context.

26.8.63

I do hope you are surviving the fury of the elements, reflecting, as it does, certain strong turbulences *'au delà'*.

In spite of the promptings of Those who use me from time to

time as their mouthpiece here below, I find myself reluctant to publish those Jesus notes; even in a suitable framework; without first seeking his own views and wishes. Usually he is accessible without great difficulty, in fact more than ready to hold out a helping hand to all those who revere and love him as an Elder Brother. Just now, however, a very important Hierarchical Council is in almost permanent session, from which he cannot free himself. No wonder! seeing that decisions are being taken about the when and where and how of what Christians refer to as the 'Second Coming'.

27.8.63

The effects of atomic explosions and their aftermath create these distressing conditions in Borderland and the lower astral. Man is a foolish creature.

Yes I am sure Carmichael's book calls for counter action. But hang it all – why should WTP write another book at all? *You* have all the material and could place the Jesus scripts in your own framework. Much better for you to have a completely free hand and (if the central character himself sees no objection) what need WTP do beyond dealing with any points of difficulty if asked by you so to do?

By the way: *à propos* of the many reports one hears of Jesus being seen and heard at séances etc. I have it on his own authority that he never manifests in this way and never will. Hallucination and self-deception account for these alleged appearances.

Later. I got a message through to the Secretary of the Conference referred to in my last. He kindly made enquiries at the Source, the reply being to refer me to one well known to me as a high official in the Michael Hierarchy (Preparers of the Way). He too passed my enquiry higher up. Having a keen sense of humour and knowing my allergy to many Vatican methods he gave me the reply: 'Nihil Obstat'.

I take this to mean we can proceed, but that whatever is published about the past should be linked in some way with what is being prepared in the near future. One level of my mind regards all this with caution: for *who are we* to be entrusted thus?

In any case it is a source of great satisfaction to me that Alexias possesses an agile and understanding mind, yet fairly stable and blessed with protective humour.

30.8.63

Now let me see; what is there to pass on to you today? 'Nihil Obstat' gives us our freewill. It we proceed, we should bear in mind Jesus' own passionate interest in furthering all possible methods for harmonizing life on this planet in all its forms. I feel that you should set your sights to reach a wider public than books on spiritualism or psychics can command, avoiding the associated jargon. But who am I to teach my granddaughter to suck eggs?

Dr. Rolf. I may try to see her again before she leaves. And may then presume to indicate the point in the human etheric structure at which terrestrial gravitational force pulling downwards meets spiritual gravitational energy pulling in the opposite direction. Complete poise of mind and body depends upon the way in which these opposing forces is balanced (within what one might call the etheric solar plexus).

The principle of the Triad within the atom, as set forth very sketchily in *The Enigma of Good versus Evil*, illustrates the thesis.

1.9.63

Well Alexias what a fascinating life you lead! Escorted here and there by famous devoted friends, lunching with cheetahs, dining with your illustrious brother, consorting with the Queen of Greece, Princes and Dukes, fêted by the literary élite. Remarkable to have earned all this and I am more than delighted at the variety of your experiences and contacts.

Jesus surrounds himself still with very simple people, many of whom might even fall into the category you have wisely assigned to you and me, namely *'worms'*. It is rarely the seemingly likely people who are chosen for his work.

As to Magic. 'White' magic is the operation of spiritual law in human affairs, unobstructed by man-made friction and ignorance. It is natural and will ultimately become universal in operation (when the Golden Age dawns). Man-made magic, largely processed by ritual, blood-letting, sexual practices unharnessed, the chanting of mantras and so on – is *not* in line with evolutionary progress. It is dependent largely on the use of astral fluids, that can be potent but are entirely unstable and therefore unreliable. Neither Jesus nor any other great Initiate ever descended to the use of such practices.

3.9.63

If you go on like a good girl for the next twenty-five or thirty years I don't see why, with luck, you should not be able to wriggle through the Golden Gates into comparative security. However I must not allow undue optimism to run away with me, even on your account.

I get tired of rising at six a.m. in order to reach London by 9.15, even if only for three or four days a week. On the other hand, good night air is a blessing, and also the fact that in the country from April to end of October one can fill the house with one's own freshly cut flowers.

Have been studying my diary for first twelve days of October. As I do so, the inked-in list of engagements becomes transparent. This usually means that I must be prepared to cancel everything for the period in question, for a call elsewhere (usually abroad). Time will tell. One learns in the end to live 'loosely', by which I mean – well, you know what I do *not* mean.

5.9.63

Delightful to have children around you. Blow your trumpet whenever the spirit moves; even if 'raps' may follow. Meanwhile I will tell you something (as if I were not doing this nearly all the time!).

When Simone S.C. wrote to tell me that she had suggested to you that you contact WTP, the latter said to himself: 'Why should she bother? She has a lovely home, masses of friends and a brilliant mind. Surely enough? And you did not respond to S.S.C's hint. One of my people did, though: he told me that there was a lonely vacuum in a corner of your life, waiting to be filled. And that you spent far too much time in it. However I continued to wait. . . . Then, almost as a command came: 'Take the initiative, for at least you can point out the direction for Alexias to follow; out of which a large measure of the loneliness will depart.' And so for once I obeyed.

And now for some news! Next month (D.V.) intensive research will begin in one of the best equipped laboratories on the Continent, based exclusively on WTP's findings concerning the cause of cancer and entirely new ways of overcoming it. If Destiny decrees that Man is now ready (even a minute minority) to be shown the path to lifting this curse, then . . . we shall see what we shall see. If my pocket is emptied once more in the process – well, it has happened so often before, and *blessed be* WTP always pops up again smiling, he hasn't yet started selling matches in the street. So keep your fingers crossed and your whole being in prayer. You are the only person who knows. Should I have told you? It is a mark of very real trust, indeed of comradeship.

Memo

Jesus Scripts. I am anxious not to speculate on the meaning of various N.T. contradictions, unless and until some authoritative information about them reaches me. Some time since, when the 'Upper Room' glimpse arrived, it was intimated that the most accurate account of the Supper and the teachings on that occasion was dictated by John to Polycarp, when John was a very old man living in his island retreat. These writings, I gathered, were carefully inscribed on parchment and wax scrolls and found their way, after Polycarp's passing, into the hands of the Christian community in Athens; and were eventually smuggled into Rome. Much later, they were lost or mislaid, having meanwhile been circulated to believers in Smyrna and Antioch. Ultimately they came into possession of the Empress Helena; and then later, formed part of the great library assembled by the first Emperor Justinian. And in my view they are still extant.

That the truth should be veiled and even distorted as centuries passed was not the original intention. However even the contradictions and discrepancies associated with the Gospel records have been brought into service, against the day when 'all these truths shall be uncovered'.

As to the Temple incident: Jesus spoke out so strongly, that after he had passed out into the Courtyard some of his over-zealous followers went back and without his direct sanction began to overturn the tables, conflict with the money-changers etc., thereby creating such a commotion that the Temple Guard intervened to restore order. Some of those responsible made their escape, others were captured and punished. These untoward events were a cause of great concern to the Master, and were responsible for his being followed and closely watched thereafter, both by Jewish and Roman authorities.

Insofar as the keeping of written records was concerned, this was not customary in Jesus' days. All that personally concerned him was that his teaching and life work for the Christ should be 'inscribed in Heaven', that is, indelibly imprinted upon the indestructible Akashic Records of life. These, I have been informed, will be made available in a visual manner to those who are attuned 'in the Latter Days'. For this reason trained seers are already able to begin their interpretation.

During lunch yesterday (Saturday) my little genie popped into view, and in genial mood (for him!). We have only one post in on Saturdays and I can't be bothered to go to the village P.O. in the afternoon to fetch any further correspondence there may be. However my good little lucky man said there was a letter waiting for me – 'Go and get it'. I enquired 'Who from?' Reply 'From someone on an island who interests me'. 'Why?' I asked. 'Oh because it is a builder of bridges and a filler of gaps.' For reasons unknown to me, humans of the female brand are anathema to my little man and are always referred to as 'it'. Anyway he was right, otherwise yours of Friday would not have reached me until Monday 7 p.m.

How I do waste your time by reporting such trivialities. Why don't you squash me flat? You are the first person who has ever worried about worrying me! I can't get over it. One in ten thousand.

Your optimism about the outcome of our joint effort came as a refresher on returning from receiving many of the Zürich 'plane victims into our Refuge Station. Sometimes I am borne into the ground by the burden of seeming pain and tragedy, the fears and loneliness of the countless those with whom I am called upon to deal. Well . . . Well, *that* gives you a splendid opportunity to get your own back by castigating me for an outburst of shocking self-pity.

I wish your Biro had ink in it.

When the time is ripe (for you) all that is best in your Egyptian pasts will be recovered, renewed and utilized. Youngsters like you cannot believe in the virtue of patience. You see, at 99 I can afford to be didactic: and mischievous too. So you are warned. And now back must I go to the Refuge Station. Give me a helping hand, and bless you.

10.9.63

Lovely to be with children and able to meet them on their own level. Lucky you! My grandchildren are scattered, not easily accessible, but they are all jolly youngsters.

Sunday Times cutting enclosed: how the Left is pushing forward the denigration of Jesus and his works and mission. Do my letters differ in detail from the typescript, which latter was based on memory? How on earth can a book be made from such scraps? You will be a magician to do this!

I have the copy of an inventory in Russian, from the ninth-century archives of an Orthodox Monastery near Kiev (now destroyed by the Bolsheviks). My copy is partial, translated into bad French and some Latin. A Russian comrade long ago did the translation for me, on the spot. An amazing document and contains a list of the scrolls etc., and precious objects and jewels collected by the Emperor Justinian the Great; and in my vision still extant but buried. I will show it to you and you will thrill and stagger and be enthralled. I must look it up to see whether all Polycarp's memoirs etc., were on wax, or copper or mica plates. John never learned to read or write.

The description of the pearls, diamonds, emeralds and sapphires, golden breastplates and other ornaments is wonderful, quite apart from hundreds of scrolls, both early Christian and pre-Christian. Being from a princely family in past times you will recognize some of the items. And to think that I have been within forty yards of the secret rock-hewn chamber where they still await recovery!

I must comment on your queries another time. Ladies are *so* curious; no wonder my genie calls them ITS.

I found yours of the day before yesterday when I got home last night. It is grievous that another seemingly tragic situation should descend upon you and upon a very dear friend of yours. How long! How long will it be before the Race can rise sufficiently in vision to accept with understanding the ceaseless and inevitable ebb and flow, the two-way traffic in and out of bodily form, that never stops. We cannot judge the whys and the wherefores of the inscrutable ways of Destiny, the Karmic Law that cannot be stayed until both Love and Justice have been fulfilled. What we can and must do is to keep an even keel, refuse to sink down into despair either for our loved ones or for ourselves.

I too am somewhat similarly involved just now, on behalf of nephews who are now orphans. Good that you are with children and can gather strength from their innocence and lively spirit. At this juncture my last letter must have met a poor reception. We can but live the day, from day to day, and do the best we know. I will hold the four of them and you in my thoughts and prayers.

Later. Remember that to extract a friend from the twilight of grief one must not enter into it too deeply oneself, or one only extends and strengthens its range and power. We have to try to radiate Light into these grey regions, by prayer, love and understanding. We cannot do so if we try to share the twilight by plunging into it out of sympathy and good nature.

Much love and sympathy now and always. Our Refuge Station is involved in this latest air crash near Perpignan. All English except the Plane's staff.

I hope my very dear one that you find all well on your return. You have learnt a hard lesson, slowly and very painfully over the years. Namely that the luxury of self-centred grief, 'walking in the twilight', not only engenders mental and physical depression; but actually retards the progress and well-being of the loved one for whom you grieve. To help others similarly placed one must walk in the sunlight and pour its radiance into the twilight regions where grief, resentment and self-centred sorrows abide. This cannot be done if one descends oneself.

I can make myself free for an hour on Wed.y or Friday next, when we should discuss how to lay the foundations for joint operations.

You speak about retaining letters. I receive about two hundred a week and must deal personally with most of them. If I kept letters, pantechnicons would be needed to house them.

My genie is completely unaffected by the spectacle of human antics and frailties. His work lies mainly in the realm of Nature and the carrying out of Nature's Laws. Had he not been instructed to do so by the Leader of his Lodge, I don't suppose he would ever have entered my life and environment. He is not amenable to human requests nor sensitive to needs; but has learnt to pay *some* attention to my wishes.

Justinian. Yes you shall see the Inventory. The railway track now lies above where I was tunnelling, and the Turkish authorities refused to allow me to proceed. By far the greatest tragedy of my present life.

From Oct. 2–11 I shall be incommunicado (some 3,000 miles to cover). No wonder when I looked, fifteen days ago, at my early October engagements in my diary, they all disappeared!

17.9.63

Friday 2.15.   I will bring the inventory, the story of how WTP helped Emperor Constantine V to secrete the treasure AD 778, during the siege of the city, how he and the Palace Guard which I commanded were all killed, the secret of the hiding place dying with them. One object for your study of these documents is an exercise in arousing your own memories. Persual will move you more than anything else in your life so far, apart from Sally's passing.

Your troubled friend. Sad all this intense introspection. It's like enlarging to giant size a not very clear snapshot and then allowing it to absorb one emotionally. In its own time and way the Spirit buds and blossoms through the mind, soul and body. Artificial efforts to pluck out into maturity the petals clasped within the tightly-closed bud can be disastrous. Let the process be natural, orderly, harmonious. There is plenty of time. *Still* the self and let the Light shine in. All this concentrated concern for one's own soul development is egotism. We should give up worrying about our own personal salvation. Live the day, serve others daily, forget oneself! This is the road to the real Self – and BE AT PEACE.

How can you convey all this to him?

24.9.63

No need for you to read up Byzantine history so-called. The necessary knowledge can be found within. However I send you George Young's simple record, with the warning that no date before the Conquest can be relied upon. Gregorian, Julian, Assyrian calendars confuse the issues; the death of Constantine V for instance is three years out and the whole story of his last year is lost to 'history'. His Empress was well above average and not the demon she is often depicted. I want you to dip into the well of your own memory uninfluenced by external information.

Bless you and enjoy your Scottish interlude, you will need it. The sequence of events following the recovery of the Cup at Avalon in 1906 shows a clear pattern of development:

1907. Meeting Cardinal Gasquet at Chalice Well and seeking through him to secure a record of the Cup's history in the Vatican Library. A long story. Decision to purchase the Chalice Well property when available.

1908.   First visit to Constantinople, based on WTP's psychometry from the Cup. Location of the ruins of Justinian's house. The Young Turkish Revolution supervened.

1909.   Fruitless search through European Museums etc., in attempt to identify the Cup.

1911.   Second visit to Constantinople and underground examinations of the catacombs around the Imperial Palaces on the hill and around and beneath the Santa Sophia.

1913.   Third visit of reconnaissance.

1914/18.   War preoccupations.

1919.   Formation in Egypt of the Quest Group. Three Russians, two English and one French scholar (female); a Byzantine expert. (All now gone save WTP.)

1920.   Quest Group at Constantinople.

1921.   Recovery of the Inventory. Reconstruction and re-living of the events of AD 778.

1922/30.   Continued but sporadic research at C. and elsewhere.

1930/35.   Negotiations at Ankara to secure a concession for archaeological exploration. A costly and lengthy process!

1937.   Securing of the concession under the auspices of the Walker Trust of St. Andrews University.

What a pattern! Leading where? I don't suppose I shall return to Constantinople in this life. Thrice have I faced death there, twice underground and once in daylight or rather night light.

25.9.63

As to the Quest, you now know enough of the situation to realize that it must go on. I dare not be the last link in an uncompleted chain. Nor if you are drawn in can *you*. I am not clever enough to write a book of true facts in the form of a fable. Are you? Should we be searching already for a third link to make up a Triad and so ensure some measure of Quest continuity? Guidance will come.

. . .

The sun is now shining and so I hope its Light is also within and around you.

68

A very hurried line to thank you for yours from Peebles. No wonder you are puzzled about dates. AD 1453 would seem to fit so much better than AD 778.

One historian writes that Constantine Vth's end was obscure and that he may have died violently in conflict. He was anti-clerical and the Ecclesiastics were constantly intriguing against him. *They* were responsible for letting the subsidized rabble through the Golden Gate which I was defending. The city's downfall may have been temporary only, Constantinople constantly changed hands over the centuries.

Had the date been 15th century the description of fighting methods would have shown them to be less primitive. Also if the treasure had remained extant and known until then there would have been documentary reference to it.

This book is considered to be a priority (I don't know why; but those concerned desire certain seeds to be sown in human consciousness NOW, of a kind we are considered competent both to generate and to sow). I will fit my dates to yours between 13 Nov. and 10 Dec. And so it is for you to call the tune.

If you use the word 'death' in reference to the house and not its occupant, well and good. Actually it is incorrect to speak even of the 'death' of the physical body, for it dissolves into a thousand energies and emanations, even when cremated. To say nothing of its central core which is absorbed into the soul's mental form or 'body'. Sooner or later this core provides the crux or foundation for the same soul's next incarnating form.

I will let you into a secret. There are powers and principalities dedicated to bringing about the total disappearance of individual life as we understand it. They work for the dissolution of the human soul's individuality in the Ocean of Life unmanifest, to precede an entirely new era of evolution in fresh patterns. To this end these Powers co-operate with man in his efforts to destroy himself via nuclear explosions, the misuse of his freewill and so on.

They are unlikely to succeed. But whenever we use the word 'death' we provide ammunition for the use of these Powers. Now that the race is striving to launch itself on the upward arc, the poetical grandeur of 'Death' must be exchanged for the sheer majesty of Life indestructible.

10.11.63

Remember that etheric storms and astral turbulences cannot touch those who have not aligned themselves by way of mediumistic communications. The latter can assuage grief at times despite the uncertainties of reception, but until one learns to live in mind and emotion in the blue sky above Borderland one must expect to be subject to depressions and magnetic convulsions. From *above* these we can help those we love, and serve far more effectively than by trying to contact them through spiritualistic practices, however attractive and easy these may seem to be. Hard lines that I am so severe about this.

19.11.63

Memo

The Cup. In my view this Cup came to light when it did for three main purposes.
(i) To act symbolically as a herald of the New Age when the Cross of suffering and discord will be replaced by the Chalice of joy and unity.

(ii) To point the way toward the recovery of 1st century Christian records.

(iii) To ensure the preservation of the Chalice Well spring and property (by purchase), the gateway through which the Christ message first reached our Island and the West and from which it was proclaimed; and to prepare C.W. for similar use at this juncture in human affairs.

However, the Cup's *known* story has no satisfactory beginning, middle or end – or at least no end yet in sight. How then can its narrative be presented without giving the impression of yet another mysterious and inconclusive psychic episode? To leave out all references to the Quest is an emasculation, yet it must be done. Mention of the Cup everywhere excites curiosity, sensation and controversy; if the forthcoming book* in all its other aspects is to be placed in the shade by the Cup story, then we shall have failed of our purpose.

22.11.63

Memo

References to the etheric body are current in occult literature and the term is also widely used within the spiritualist movement. As the writer sees it, 'double' or 'counterpart' is the better word. This double which fits the physical form like a glove is not the vehicle used by man when he passes into another and wider realm of consciousness at 'death'. During earth life the invisible substance of which this double is constructed acts as a link between the mind and the brain, and so between the physical expression of man and his Ego or real Self.

This etheric counterpart does not long survive the dissolution of the physical body and, having fulfilled its functions, the force it contains is reabsorbed into the general reservoir of energy from

* *A Man Seen Afar.*

71

which it originated, to re-emerge in due course for use again. During this process, any man-made impurities accumulated (the result of discordant thinking and feeling) drop away, so that the source is uncontaminated. These impurities appear to crystallize into an opaque sediment which then forms part of the hard core of unmanifested matter that acts as a curtain or barrier between our world and the invisible realms. As man progresses this barrier will gradually disappear.

The body with which we are clothed on quitting the physical form at 'death' is formed of a substance to which the term 'etheric' should not be applied. Whilst the etheric double (so useful to us during earth life) is built up from the primary elements which constitute air and water (as we know them), man's new body is free from such material associations, of different construction and more spiritual elements. The term 'astral' is used to describe this body, in an attempt to differentiate terrestrial substance and that which originates 'in the stars', that is, from more spiritual sources.

Language is not framed to convey accurate ideas of conditions prevailing in realms of consciousness beyond our three-dimensional level of life and being: I am well aware of the inadequacy of such attempts at description.

Returning to a consideration of the etheric double and its uses: I think that other research workers in this field will confirm my thesis that methods of communication between ourselves and those no longer with us, such as trance mediumship, automatic writing, hypnotism, require the use of etheric substance. These methods I would clearly distinguish from telepathy, the direct communion between mind and mind, for which the capacity is latent in us all, and through the use of which the barriers of time and space can be safely broken down. I am persuaded that *this* form of communion is spiritual in origin. It appears to fulfil rather than retard the working of spiritual Law. On the other hand, is there good reason to believe that the operations of this Law are interfered with by the exploitation of etheric substance? I will try to answer this question very tentatively, claiming no authority to dogmatize.

Let us consider the case of those who leave this world spiritually unenlightened, and unwilling, perhaps, to depart. (Do not be too sure that many of us are not in this category!) I awake to find myself alive, but in strange surroundings. Shock, perhaps; the urge to the familiar; the desires and sorrows of those left behind, all may tend to draw me back towards the conditions I have left, and the only means by which I can achieve re-entry is by the reanimation of my only link, the etheric double. Thus I can respond to the gravitational pull downwards, or I can strive to continue my journey on the upward way. On the upward path, having allowed the etheric double to follow the physical body into dissolution as it should, I can still remain in communion with my loved ones telepathically and in such a way as to help rather than obstruct their own spiritual progress.

In my view it is unwise to linger in the Borderland region for the sole purpose of retaining etheric contact with those I have left behind. To say that it would be wrong to do so depends mainly I think on the point in evolution and enlightenment at which one stands when presented with the choice. Human evolution is an infinitely gradual process and no two individuals stand at the same point. Therefore I will not be dogmatic, since a course right for me to follow might be wrong for you to pursue. I leave you to weigh the issues before reaching your own conclusions.

24.11.63

I have read the book you lent me and here are my comments. Teachings contained in the great majority of books of this kind (of which the number and variety would seem to be without end) appear to possess one common denominator: they are occupied almost exclusively with the relation between God and man, the individual's personal destiny being regarded as of supreme importance. In this respect, communicators seem to suffer from a myopic limitation of vision. Who are we (or they) to assert that man represents the Creator's highest achievement? Why are we so sure we occupy the centre of the stage within the immensity of the spiritual universes and the solar systems known to exist?

What may become of us is of minor importance on the cosmic scale. Cannot we begin to widen our interests and our comprehension and our vision beyond the confines of self? Even apart from Angels and Archangels and all the Company of Heaven, the universe undoubtedly contains individual beings of an order quite different from our own, and who may well be more valuable than we are. Let us pray to be granted that wider vision through which the grace of humility may become ours.

In this series of communications there is no direct reference to the fact that progress or retrogression of man on this planet is dependent on the evolution and well-being of all other forms of life that share it with us within the other Kingdoms of Nature. Evolution is a tidal process. The ebb and flow of ours is inextricably bound up with similar living rhythms within the Kingdoms of Air, Water, Fire, and the Animal, Vegetable and Mineral worlds. How is it that these Teachers from Beyond can ignore this fact, with the result that their communications must add to man's deluded sense of his own pre-eminence?

One would wish that those who have preceded us to the next level of consciousness would be less eager to impart 'teachings' before they themselves really know what they are talking about. The change called death does not in itself ensure either greater enlightenment or wider vision. For this reason we on this side of the veil should remember that true understanding can be reached most surely from within ourselves as the result of prayer, silence and deep humility.

Moreover it is apparently taken for granted by these 'Teachers' that everyone born into this world is necessarily a complete entity in his or her own right. No reference is made to the thesis that a considerable number of those so born have not yet attained an independent identity, but in fact form part of a Group Soul. The thesis of such shared being solves many knotty problems associated with reincarnation. It may be that our characteristic egocentricity makes us shrink away from this and other cherished beliefs which sustain our self-esteem. It is essential however that the seeds of new ideas leading to a wider outlook be sown, and their growth enabled. In this connexion it cannot be stressed too often that the more we rely upon outside sources of spiritual enlightenment the more difficult it will be to awaken within

74

ourselves those faculties, the use of which can teach us all things we need to know.

7.12.63

Alexias my dear, try as I will to reduce the 'certain young man's' story to narrative form, I do not succeed. It comes out stilted and artificial. Yet my memory of the living experience is clear.

There was extreme urgency in the Captain of the Sanhedrin Guard's command to his legionary to pursue, capture alive and bring back the youth who after touching Jesus on the breast had burst his way out through the milling throng and dashed up Mount Scopus; crying out and lamenting loudly all the way.

Apparently one of the priests present feared a plot to rescue Jesus, and imagined that in some way this youth must be implicated in it.

Before starting in pursuit Kopul slung the linen garment over his shoulder, having first shed his mail and heavy boots in order to be free to move more swiftly. As it turned out the light sandals he had hastily put on soon filled with small stones as he raced through the olive groves and up on to the rocky bare hillside, and much impeded his progress. To one who at that moment happened to be riding within the mind of the pursuer, incidents connected with the chase left an indelible impression. Not easy to describe. It was as if the linen garment were acting as a strange link between the pursuer and the pursued.

As a result, the terror and desolation which were driving the distracted youth far out into the wilderness found lodgement in Kopul's mind and heart, to the exclusion of all else. He became obsessed with the urgent need to catch up with the fugitive, to share his grief and to bring him consolation. The chase went on all through the night, down through the cactus-covered wastelands and on into the sombre valley of the Dead Sea. Shortly before dawn Kopul gave up the pursuit in despair, having lost all sense of direction in the trackless wilderness. He finally found his way back to the Garden, limping and exhausted, overcome by a sense of purpose unfulfilled. . . .

The rest of the story you already have. I am very sorry I have been unable to relate these events with fluency; but tragic memory of them seems to paralyse my pen.

I really wondered what had become of you over Christmastide. Apparently you lay hidden from view (and from the Light) in a pocket of depression and unease. Usually I can pick you up wherever you are, largely because my horizons happen to extend well beyond the limits of yours, and so embrace them. It was not a happy Christmas despite the usual plethora of festivities and tinsel in the western world. It is a sad time too for Jesus to watch a celebration nominally of his arrival on our planet turned into an orgy of pagan gorging on millions of slaughtered creatures.

I have recently been with one of those lucky(?) people who manage to go through life tranquilly, accepting whatever comes along; serenely untouched by tragedy or the stress of external circumstance. In her own circle —— is regarded as a Saint: and yet how much she has missed in deep mental and emotional experience! Pain, doubt, fear, distress for the sorrows of the world, grief for the little one can do to allay and solace its ills: all this lies outside her horizons. As is the case with so many good and warm-hearted people whose warmth is static.

Anyway I do hope you are now recovering, stoking up your courage and all inner resources to face perhaps the most important and valuable year of your life (so far). It will be a treat to renew acquaintance with *Uncle Vanya* in your company. *Good* of you to give me the chance.

I had hoped to be allowed to 'see' much over Christmastide but a curtain was pulled down, and so I accepted this as a signal of protection. Vision can be painful as well as inspiring and no one should try to carry heavier burdens than can be borne without risk of breakdown.

I am relying now on memory rather than on the capacity to re-live an experience in which I have been concerned. This incident in which Judas was involved happened one bitter winter evening during the second year of Jesus' public ministry.

A protégé of mine at that time was a Syrian lad of eighteen (Reuben by name) who showed signs of becoming a very remarkable singer and musician. Never before or since have I heard such a strong, clear and lovely tenor voice. (His parents were old friends of mine and I had helped to finance his training.)

His home was near Damascus, but on the occasion to which I am now referring this young man had come down to meet me in Capernaum where I happened to be staying at the time. (I was not a Jew, by the way!) On this evening I had invited a few friends to join me at the inn where I was lodged to give them the pleasure of hearing Reuben's glorious voice. One of these good friends of mine brought Judas the Iscariot with him, the latter having a keen ear for music: I had met him only twice before, when he impressed me as being a man of culture and intelligence.

When the party was breaking up Judas took me on one side, saying he would like to be allowed to ask my advice. He then showed me a piece of gold and, knowing I was an authority on Roman coinage, asked me its origin and value. It turned out to be a specimen of a medallion struck by the City of Rome for presentation to those who received the Freedom of the City in return for deeds of valour and outstanding service. Judas then told me that this coin had been given to him by Mary Magdalene, only the night before, for the purpose of buying a warm cloak for Jesus, who, he told me, was staying near Capernaum at this time. Late in the afternoon two days before, Jesus had been asked to go up into the hills behind the town to rescue a shepherd boy who had broken his leg, and who, after suffering exposure for several days before he was found, was too ill to be moved. Everyone in Galilee knew the immense love Jesus cherished towards shepherds and all who had the care of animals. Judas told me he was with Jesus when the summons came, and that he arranged for two of the boy's older brothers to accompany Jesus, carrying with them a rough wooden stretcher. Two members of the household where Jesus was staying, but whose names I do not remember, also went as guides and helpers. When Jesus reached the spot he took off his cloak and wrapped the half-conscious boy in its ample folds. It was then that the miracle happened.

According to the subsequent report of those present, no stretcher was needed, for the boy stood up in full possession of his senses, his broken leg became straight and he was able to climb down the rugged mountain tracks unaided. Having blessed the lad and arranged for one of his brothers to mind the sheep, Jesus sent the boy home still wearing his cloak.

Later when Mary Magdalene was told of what had happened, she gave Judas the gold coin and begged him to sell it to provide Jesus with a new cloak. She told Judas that this medallion had been given to her as a parting gift by a Roman officer, the most precious friend she had ever had. Nothing but the thought of Jesus cloakless on that bitter winter night would have induced her to part with it.

Judas then told me that as the community purse was empty and Joseph the Arimathean absent overseas, he felt obliged to accept the gift and renewed his request that I should find a buyer for the medallion, which could not be used as currency. I explained that it would be contrary to Roman law to barter or sell a gold piece of this description and that at all costs it should be returned to the giver forthwith. I then remembered that a very warm camel hair cloak had been given to me by my father as a present on my reaching manhood and that I had hardly worn it since. I sent my servant to fetch it from my home near Jerusalem, with instructions to give it to Mary so that she could adjust its length to suit Jesus' figure. Memory fades at this point. However, I do remember with great joy that when I met Jesus some time later my cloak was around his shoulders.

There is a strange sequel to this story, one that took place nearly nineteen hundred years later.

In the early winter of 1919 I was walking on Mount Carmel with the great Persian prophet Abdul Baha Abbas, a 'man of God', of great spiritual stature; he noticed that I was suffering from the cold. Immediately he took off the camel hair cloak he was wearing and placed it over my shoulders (it was mine for keeps). (It was then he made the cryptic remark that I was destined to become a

'Joseph in my own land'.) I had forgotten the incidents related in these notes and therefore could not understand what the wind seemed to be whispering in my ears: 'Restitution after many days. . . .'

Had it not been for the example of Judas' fall from grace, subsequent remorse and suicide, almost the whole of early Christian history would have been different and far less valuable. The courage of many early martyrs was based (indirectly) on the lesson taught by the Judas tragedy.

N.B. When one re-lives an incident from the past one can relate it spontaneously and accurately. But when one tries to record long past events from memory, there are gaps in one's recollection and spontaneity is lost.

6.1.64

Sorry that the notes sent to you about Judas etc., were such a jumble, but one's memory ebbs and flows in ways that do not make for coherence.

Reuben's father was a Syrian merchant but his mother came of a Hebrew farming family in Galilee. And it was she who insisted on their only son being given a Jewish name.

I do not pretend to know why Judas fell from grace. Nor why, when Jesus marked him out at the Supper, the other disciples did not take him into custody to prevent the betrayal. However somewhere sometime I seem to have heard Jesus' words in this context – 'Suffer him to go'. *Judas was aware of another plot by brigand revolutionaries to abduct Jesus and he may have felt that he would be safer in the protective hands of the authorities; having no idea that a capital charge was pending.*

Whether his being used as a tool of Destiny would lessen his own karmic burden is a problem for the metaphysicians!?

The pristine springs associated with the ministry of Christ through Jesus are in process of being re-opened (for use by Jesus' successor and also by those now preparing his way). 1964 therefore *must* witness the publication of the *Jesus glimpses* as being an essential portion of the tapestry now being so carefully woven. We knew this over four months ago. Other priorities and perplexities have intervened. Time is now running on and out (and they are *my* knuckles that are now being rapped, not yours). If you feel this to be an impossible task, with all the other commitments that face you, *do not* force issues: in that case I will get going on a collection like *The Silent Road*, but to include the Jesus incidents. Your Foreword would be more than deeply valued.

And now for your questions. Akhenaten was (and is) an Adept whose aura is both powerful and extensive. Some of those who were near him over 3,500 years ago became so fully impregnated with the radiations from this aura that clairvoyants have sensed the influence and jumped unwisely to wrong conclusions.

Very few of the Jesus sites so-called are historically correct. For instance the house (long since destroyed) containing the Upper Room was not at the summit of Mt. Zion where a tumbledown church exists, but a long way down its eastern slope.

If one wishes to comprehend the full beauty of a drop of dew, or of a rose bud, or of an emerald, one needs to pierce beneath the surface, to extend one's sight inwards to the heart of the object. 'Looking within' however is not concerned with one's physical form. And this kind of looking being four-dimensional implies a 'within' that has nothing to do with time, space or form. The gateway to spiritual awareness lies within the mind, not the brain, the heart or any part of the body. One method for reaching up to this gateway within the mind is touched upon in *The Silent Road* chapter on Imagination.

Also it is a good plan when sitting in the Silence, fully relaxed, to dwell in thought on one of the primary qualities of Deity. Try to visualize this quality as it is possible for man to manifest its virtue to his fellows. Then use this visualization as a gateway for passing out beyond the confines of your conscious mind into a state of superconsciousness. An extension of awareness can follow within

which one's questions are answered and one's soul finds consolation and peace.

Judas. There is much about him and his place in the cosmic drama
which, for reasons unknown to me, cannot be released for
publication at this juncture. This applies also to many of the major
happenings in Jesus' own life on earth.

One problem facing anyone who tries to share experiences, is
that he needs to be very sure he does not knock away props before
he can provide more reliable spiritual supports acceptable to those
who cannot stand on their own feet. Maybe this is why so much of
import concerned with events in Palestine between AD 15 and
AD 33 is still being withheld.

I agree with what you say about the feeble flabbiness of so much
'other-worldly' communication. This is on a par with the attempt to
turn Jesus and other Masters into effeminate characters and to
make a wishy-washy mixture of religion. You speak as if you
thought WTP would be upset if you were not 'convinced' by what
he tells you: what *would* upset me would be for you to accept as
truth everything I say just because I say it! Recognition of truth
comes from within, and until this happens it is only belief and not
conviction that applies. So it seems to me.

Jesus was greatly handicapped by not being allowed to cast his
pearls more widely and more publicly when here 2,000 years ago.
His prophetic vision was clear that the human race had to fall yet

further into materialism and sensuality before an upward swing in the evolutionary cycle could begin. Man was destined to drain to the dregs the cup he himself had filled with sorrow, suffering, selfishness, greed, envy, fear and every conceivable sexual and emotional excess. (On the mystery of the inference that the upward climb can only be started from the lowest depths, one knows of men who have wilfully experienced every possible sexual and other debasement, as the prerequisite of their subsequent upward progress.) It would have been useless for Jesus to give out to the multitude more than they could accept: he could but give the simplest teaching, leavened with the principles on which all Life processes and progressions are based. He was well aware that to his successor would fall the task of revelations far beyond and above any that he himself was allowed to impart.

There is an esoteric tradition to the effect that on an occasion during Jesus' thirty-first year on earth, when speaking to a hostile crowd outside the Damascus Gate (on market day), words in the following sense were heard above the general din by a few close to him:

> I say unto you:
> Whatever your deeds may be,
> Let them be done in My Name:
> That you may enter the Kingdom
> And find rest.

Of course Jesus never made utterances of this kind on his own responsibility. The 'My' denoted the eternal Christ by whom Jesus was overshadowed on such occasions.

As in so many of the Sayings which have come down to us, there is a depth of meaning in that just quoted which far transcends the words employed. We are to bring 'The Christ' right down into every detail of our lives; we are commanded to imprint 'My Name' on everything we do – on eating and drinking, our conversations and communications, our business and our recreations; all our acts of living and of loving, whether low or exalted, whether sinful or enlightened – in fact NOTHING is to be thought, said or done that does not receive this imprimatur by an act of our will and obedience. Then, by Divine Grace even our sins can become stepping-stones out of our darkness into the light of a new day.

Memo

Glastonbury. My sister will hope to be at Wednesday's meeting and to make herself known to you afterwards.

As an item of interest you may care to mention that with the consent of the National Trust the C.W. Trust will be carrying out excavations on the upper levels of Michael Tor next August; to uncover the foundations of a Celtic chapel and also to explore for a Druid circle and altar.

The Tor hill was part of the property of the Abbots of Glastonbury and adjoins the Chalice Well gardens, which also belonged to the Benedictines up to the time of Henry VIII, Little St. Michael House being a place of retreat for the Abbot and senior monks.

A curious thing about the Cup photos. Those taken by the Museum are lustreless and dead. The ones taken hand-held instead of isolated, are alive and radiating.

Whenever Jesus handled a jar of wine or oil, or a cup or platter, these objects and their contents became scintillating as if inspired and transformed. How lovely hands can be! How ugly and even terrible, some! Sure guides to character.

Well, as I realize that I shall be given no peace until I have further touched upon the Judas enigma, I will begin to jot down some rough notes to follow this screed (with luck!).

It was I think Jesus' deep and indestructible serenity which influenced one most. Even standing 'afar off' (in comprehension) one could perceive that the basis for this serenity was a complete certainty: a certainty that embraced the knowledge that an Infinity of Love and Wisdom ruled the universe, against which nothing could prevail. It was as if he gave those around him access to a reservoir of Love in which all could bathe with joy and be cleansed and made young again.

Then there was a supreme naturalness in all he said or did, accompanied by a wonderfully illumined simplicity. When he returned from retreat or meditation the light radiating from him gave the impression of bodily translucence. From miles away one could feel the power of his aura. But when he was near, one felt uplifted to such an extent that everyone and everything around one seemed to be transformed and enlightened. It was only when anger or grief overtook him that one became aware of a Majesty that rendered him remote, unapproachable and awe-inspiring.

To watch him with children and with birds and animals was a revelation of what pure and selfless love can be. At such times all one's own joys and sorrows were swallowed up in a peace which is created by the knowledge that all is supremely well.

At such times one becomes entirely free from self and at one with all Life and Being. No words can express the loveliness of such an experience, one that will live with one for ever and again for evermore. Jesus made one feel at all times a sense of *companionship* with him on equal terms.

I cannot write of the Judas story from first hand experience (I was not present at the Supper). Therefore I find the Notes which I have tried to draw up for you profoundly unsatisfactory. Short of a search in the Akashic Records, which I do not feel drawn to undertake, I can best offer these comments and reminders: we are dominated by dualities down here, by the action of opposing energies: we learn to recognize 'good' by the contrasting manifestation of 'less good', or even 'evil'. It is through the missionary efforts of Lucifer that we learn to lift ourselves out of darkness into Light. Lucifer's role was an essential background to Christ's ministry on earth through Jesus: by it Darkness was used to throw

84

into constructive relief the Light of Christ's message to the human race.

13.3.64

Memo

Here is an attempt to answer your query about certain occult uses of sex to secure 'enlightenment' through the opening of the third eye.

This particular teaching derives from the very earliest forms of Indian and African magic. The human intellect alone is incapable of arousing man's creative imagination, or of bringing it into full flower, and certain forms of *psychic* development cannot be attained until this arousal has taken place. Magicians are seeking short cuts to psychic powers, through the abnormal stimulation of the imagination. Certain drugs, the specific use of alcohol, abnormal breathing exercises, are amongst these artificial methods. The mind should always be in full control of the imagination, but these artificial stimuli reverse the process, so that the mind ceases to be master and becomes slave. And sex can be used for the same purpose.

To empty oneself in order to be filled from the Divine Reservoir is a process under mental control, and one to be strongly encouraged (with due safeguards): on the other hand the expedient of emptying oneself emotionally by the forcible expulsion of the seminal fluids both physical and etheric can lead to lunacy, and at best can only induce illusory and sensual dreams, which state is the exact opposite of spiritual enlightenment.

Orderly evolution and the striking of the correct balance between the use of the mind and the emotions lead *naturally* to a point where spiritual potential unfolds; then psychic vision, to the extent needed (if at all) becomes the natural corollary and handmaiden of spiritual seership.

A bit of good news, to cheer you up. Since the Arthur Courtyard at Chalice Well has been regenerated, the avenue between it and its astral counterpart has been reopened. Invaluable energies are now flowing in both directions once more. One result is that a healing oasis in Borderland has come into useful being between the two; to the great benefit of many lost and lonely souls and other distracted wanderers – *Laus Deo!*

Eastertide 1964

Memo

As a duty more than a pleasure I have been listening to Good Friday sermons and Radio discourses, mainly concerned with the enormity of our sins and stressing how little we deserve salvation. I don't believe such talk tends to make us better people?

I note that most of the current theologians still believe that St. John of the Gospel was the 'beloved disciple' at the Cross. In which case why does the author of John's Gospel speak of 'that disciple' and not in the first person?

I was not there in the flesh and there is a subtle difference in the quality of memory between events experienced and those reported. Hence I apply the word 'glimpses' to what one *saw* rather than to what one thought or heard about.

Personally I regard the stories of the fig tree and the swine as apocryphal, and symbolical. As to the swine, they were frightened by a cloudburst which so far as I am aware was purely coincidental: true they raced down a narrow ravine and were lost to sight, but it was miles from the sea! No one amongst the few onlookers could read or write, the story they told passed therefore from mouth to mouth and from village to village with the usual exaggerations and interpolations.

Let me tell you a fragment from a story which illustrates my meaning.

In 1918 I was instrumental in seeing that measures were taken to safeguard the lives of the Persian prophet Abdul Baha and his family, from possible martyrdom by the Turks, when we were besieging Haifa and closing in on Mount Carmel, where the Bahais had their settlement. What I did could have been done by anyone else in my position (as a Staff Major in Intelligence). That took place fifty years ago, but the incident has become in Persia and India a miraculous legend which converts me into a Saint endowed with celestial prowess and seership of the first order. True believers are shown the exact spot where the gallows was being erected for the execution of their Master, whom they regard as equal in spiritual stature to Jesus. Now if in our times, with our Press, with photography, and a large measure of literacy, an historical incident can be so transformed, and within fifty years of the event . . . what could not have happened in the century or more after Jesus' time, in the portrayal of what he said and did?

First, hearsay; then written down, then copied from Aramaic into Hebrew, Greek and Latin. Then re-copied and annotated, over and over again, each scribe adding his own gloss. The wonder is that we are left with anything at all that can be called authentic.

Coming back to our muttons, I don't want to create needless confusion in that very perceptive mind of yours: I mean, by drawing a distinction in value between glimpses of what I myself saw and took part in; and what was told me at the time – hearsay; or what I reasoned out as being the probable truth. Nevertheless the distinction is important. Watching Jesus poised to dive into the Jordan, or perched up in an olive tree, is one thing. Trying to explain who was or who was not present on a given occasion when I was not myself present, is quite another. Many of the questions you have posed deal with events of which I have had no first hand experience. In these conditions any clairvoyant deductions of mine may be subject to error, and should therefore be treated with caution.

24.3.64

Now about the book. The terms of reference were simple: to take all possible steps to ensure that the *Jesus glimpses* were brought into the daylight before the year closed (i.e. the solar year which ends in March next). No duty exists to try to bring conviction to readers, apparently this is not to be our concern. We have solely and very simply to sow the seeds that have been provided. Anyway I feel sure it is best now to get the existing material into typescript form and in suitable order, quite apart from what you may decide to do, or not do, over and above editing and collating.

28.3.64

National Trust

I wrote Mr. Rathbone courteously but firmly and I hope they won't insist on reserving for themselves all publicity rights connected with the Tor dig. I see the N.T. London H.Q. is at 42 Queen Annes Gate. This was the home of a great buddy of mine, a Californian beauty and one of the more respectable friends of Edward VII. Under her hospitable roof I have met Lodge, Crookes, Mark Twain, Archdeacon Wilberforce, R. J. Campbell (the famous City Temple preacher), Princess Karadja (quite a magician in her own right), Conan Doyle and the rest. What memories!

By the way some oriental mythologies regard the vine and its fruit as symbolizing spiritual enlightenment and joy. The apple or pomegranate as the container of both good and evil. And the fig as symbolizing material and sensual pleasure and knowledge. However I think the story that Jesus cursed a fig tree is pure legend. Neither Luke nor John thought this tradition worthy of mention. Jesus as an Initiate could live indefinitely on air and water. Moreover the alleged incident took place just before the Passover and so it must have been prior to March 15th. Jesus was of course well aware that in Palestine not even minute figs would be visible so early in the year: to curse a tree because it was unfruitful out of season is not an act of which he could have been capable.

88

Well here am I once more on an island which has been a focus for the Energies of the Left throughout the existence of evolutionary life on this planet. As I do *not* follow the Left Path I always keep fingers crossed when Fate brings me here. One never knows. . . . Yet from out this very dark stronghold, Light could emerge capable of lifting the cruel burden of woes under which the human race is now staggering – a burden far heavier even than the Cross carried by Jesus to Calvary.

I pay my respects to Etna's Guardians (and Stokers) . . . 'muttering' may precede another severe outburst. Yet we should all give thanks for safety valves like this one. For without them our planet would soon disintegrate.

Torrential rain has never ceased since my arrival. This is one of the ways in which the Left is venting its anxious displeasure at what the insignificant pygmy WTP is trying to do. Also 'they' made landing here by plane a touch and go affair. When I talk to my friends the Enemy I tell them not to waste time on trivia – let them send me down into Etna's boiling crater and have done with any flea bites WTP may have been able to inflict upon them. Seriously however, unless the weather improves before 20.4.64 when I leave this strangely sinister island, it will not be possible to do what I came out to attempt.

I had a spot of luck in Rome by contacting by 'hazard' a Dane whose influence may enable me to trace and perhaps recover Michel Pojidaier's bust of the Czaritza, which was sold years ago with the other effects of the Grand Duchess Olga, having been the property of the last Dowager Empress of Russia.*

My Dane farms 10,000 acres in his own land; but can only make ends meet by breeding mink for the Hudson Bay Comp.y. The thoughtless cruelty of women's fashions!

---

* So far as I know, never traced.

Rubens Hotel,
London SW1
St. George's Day 1964

Memo

I wrote you a note today from the Office, using my old and friendly pen. I can write with no other. But it seemed this was to be the last time I would be able to use it, for soon after in Victoria Street, on putting up my umbrella, the pen became dislodged from its clip and fell into the gutter. From there the running rain water carried it down one of those barred drain vents, and it disappeared. Sadly I went on my way to attend a meeting of the Tor School Governors.

At this function my daughter Jean, who is a Governor, presented me with a new fountain pen. A good one, but not my style and not easy to handle. Alas, alack! Naughtily I summoned my genie saying I wanted my old and trusted pen back.

The day passed on and nothing happened. Crossly I asked why. Quite as crossly my genie exploded: 'Give me time! You are not yet back at your hotel.'

At 9 p.m. (an hour ago) I returned here, my room having been locked all day. Undressed, put on a dressing-gown and sat down to read my evening mail. And to take some notes, with the awkward new pen. . . . Giving this up in despair, I sat back, the half written notes lying on the table before me.

Hearing a sound, I discovered that the new pen had rolled off the table on to the floor. As I stooped to retrieve it my delighted gaze spotted my dear old friend lying comfortably on the table, right across the paper on which the unfinished notes had been set down.

So I can now go to bed with a thankful heart. Despite a somewhat guilty feeling that my G. should not be used for such trifles.

26.4.64

Reference enclosed cutting: I never met Jesus or any of those around him dressed in flowing nightgowns. Beards were not worn long, save by the elderly, but very close cropped and often cut to a trim fringe only. Jesus usually wore a kind of short linen tunic, sometimes loosely belted (no buttons). Sandals, but he often went about barefoot and he possessed beautifully proportioned, strong and agile feet. Under the tunic, a fairly close-fitting second tunic, beginning at the waist and extending below the outer one to just above the knees and rarely lower. On wet rough days he often wore a camel hair hooded cloak, which sometimes he wound around him much like the habit of a lay brother in a monastery. I never met him carrying a staff, save when wearing a cloak – never for walking or climbing when cloakless and sandal-less with open tunic plus a loin cloth. Socks or stockings, anyway for men, were not worn. But one occasionally saw fine closely woven straw or fibre leggings, flesh coloured and not unlike the modern puttee. Jesus never wore amulets or rings or other ornaments. This illustration is of course imaginative and makes him look far too. elderly. When the episode illustrated took place, nearly all present were in their early thirties or even younger: and Jesus *never* lost his pristine youth and vital zest. His working followers were encouraged by him to retain the clothes of their calling.

30.4.64

The Flight into Egypt

This was before my time, some while before I had any connexion with the boyhood of Jesus, or his family. I do not doubt that this journey took place, although it is only recorded I think in St. Matthew? From time to time I had heard the story repeated and there always seemed to be some mystery about details. On one occasion I overheard a bereaved mother lamenting 'If only *They* had remained among us the Hand of the Lord would have stayed the slaughter and saved my son.'

Esoteric tradition tells of a very holy Initiate of the Egyptian School of Mysteries, whose blessing for Jesus, Joseph and Mary sought when down there. This would be a sound reason for undertaking such a journey, even when Jesus was so young.

Reincarnation
An immense and subtle subject. Very few of those now here are in *full* incarnation; that is to say, the Ego sends down a different ray from itself, one at a time, for the gaining of discipline and experience. It is for this reason that memories of past lives on earth are so very difficult to recover. Ultimately the Ego absorbs all its rays, and then when the individual's evolution on this planet is nearing completion sends down into incarnation its completed soul as a single entity.

At least thirty per cent, probably more, of those now on earth are not yet even individualized, being still parts of a group soul. There is no fixed standard by which the number of incarnations can be gauged, and this number varies in different cases, largely in accordance with the state of each Ego's development *before* the present twenty-five-thousand-year round of evolution began.

One who has started seriously on the path of selfless service can call down from the Ego whichever particular rays are needed for the work in hand.

Reincarnation. Most people hate the idea that the complete Entity does not incarnate until many separate sections have experienced a series of earthly lives. Those who in a material sense feel *complete* are the more likely to cut themselves off from communion with their Mother soul. Yet many have the urge to seek out and follow a 'Teacher', one who is, like themselves, in incarnation. I think it is in *Matthew* (Ch. 23) that Jesus roundly exhorts his followers to 'call no man your father upon the earth . . . neither be ye called masters' (or teacher, in some modern versions of the N.T.). And is all this hunting of the Guru more reprehensible than the flitting from medium to medium, intent on the same quest?

'Seek and ye shall find' should be interpreted almost exclusively as a seeking *within*; that is, a strengthening of the link between one's incarnated self and one's *whole* Self; through which a direct road is opened between man and his Creator.

How tired you must be by WTP's insistence on the importance of silence, the stilling of one's senses, the turning away from outward chaos towards that Peace which passeth understanding.

My doctors are inclined to funk injecting my solution (even diluted) direct into the patient's bloodstream. But taken orally the healing potency of the solution is largely destroyed by stomach acids. Will the accumulation of our racial karma over so many centuries *allow* progress to be made *now* on this cancer problem?

Dr. Khoury at Amman is now treating a case of advanced carcinoma of the lungs with the Etna solution, given orally. In these circumstances if alleviation or cure is effected it will be a miracle.

13.5.64

Dr. S. Khoury M.D., F.R.C.S., my brilliant Syrian specialist friend, writes me from Amman offering his full support. Even saying that my thesis about the cause of cancer lying in etheric regions is very likely to prove correct. (David TP is due there tomorrow.) Dr. K. has his own hospital and would clear a ward for cancer patients (those without means of their own), in order to test out fully the remedies I recommend. But (naturally) asks for a contribution toward the cost of this philanthropic undertaking.

7.6.64

Sexually speaking Jesus was a virgin; that is to say, 'carnal knowledge', as the legal phrase has it, lay outside his experience altogether. He would have been fully capable of taking the father's

93

part in generating offspring. Undoubtedly he was aware of the immense pressures to which most people are subjected as the result of Nature's insistent urge within them to propagate the species. However, without sexual experience, it is unlikely that he could have entered fully into understanding of the insidious compulsion of sexual temptation as known to the majority of those around him. This may explain why, as far as our records go, he had little guidance to give in this field of human activity. We may confidently expect the coming Messenger from God to throw a flood of illumination on these problems and their solutions.

10.6.64

Evidently the Left have no intention of leaving me in peace with my Etna herbal solution. Yesterday, en route to deliver a flask of the precious concentrate to my courier (for Lausanne) I was deliberately tripped up by something or somebody when crossing busy Victoria Street. My attaché case was sent flying across the road and then on to the pavement. Fortunately it was well packed and the flask inside was not broken, as I am now very short of supplies (being clamoured for widely) and the season for collecting and processing the herbs is over until early autumn.

Now enjoy the sunshine and forget *pro tem*. WTP's troublesome existence! Probably as you say I am too severe a task-master, but not half so much so as are my own task-masters!

Of course such contacts as yours with Sally via Mrs. Twigg are consoling and the cause of true happiness. The more so because the means used is a normal, natural clairvoyant one.

Have you ever collected the data given you about other-worldly conditions from all your contacts, automatic and otherwise? And as a result do you find that the horizons of your mind have been extended, well beyond the range of personal repetitive assurances? What I hope to see is an important extension of your inner perceptions.

Never have I expressed any doubt about the inspiration and value of Lady Sandys' illuminating writings! No doubt what bias I possess against automatism (on the other hand) derives from having had to deal with so much human wreckage resulting from these indulgences.

I have been puzzled all my adult life by the many attempts made to bring my present body to destruction. Such attempts now run into dozens. Those concerned are evidently expert in the use of Nature's blind forces, as well as having the power to obsess individuals to carry out their instructions. I told you how once a wild dog saved my life. Bless him. In old Stamboul, when a Turk was waiting in a doorway to jump out and knife me, I stepped by accident on a dog lying in a hole in the street. Its yelp made me lurch forward violently, and the knife missed me by several inches. Twice too, such small incidents have saved me from being poisoned. And so it has gone on year after year, a running battle between negation and friendly protective influences. One becomes inured.

It is only natural that I should have become deeply concerned by the way in which my own memories differ in so many respects from Biblical traditions. Whilst the Jesus glimpses were being received, or recovered, I had no idea that these deviations would prove so marked and at times so surprising. I live in hope that those first century records on parchment or perhaps copper plates may yet be discovered and brought out into the light of our times.

When and if this happens, which may Providence permit, can I be allowed to believe that the memories of the times of Jesus now set down will prove historically accurate? For myself I have what I feel to be good reasons for thinking that such a revelation is not only possible but more than probable, and *well* within the confines of the present century.

Yesterday you seemed almost as if you had experienced a dark night of the soul: or anyway a grey one! Everyone who has consciously set foot on the pathway of Service inevitably becomes isolated; and this, no matter how thickly surrounded by people – friends, letters, houses and streets. And 'family'. This loneliness is the price one pays for the honour, and remember that your task is fraught with significance for generations yet unborn. We should not belittle the importance of the mission entrusted to us.

It matters *not at all* should one feel backward in personal development: Eternity is available for our use. And no one is a good judge of his own attainment. Let us therefore live each day, simply and thankfully . . . and leave the rest. . . .

As to the picture you are preparing to present of WTP: avoid grandiosity. Depict one who lives mundanely, brings up a family, soldiers, engages in industry, travels, risks his life when the object justifies it, starts and runs the Big Ben Minute; takes over the Chalice Well property and administers a boys' school; writes and lectures, studies Nature's secrets. The only way in which his life diverges from the normal run of lives is that he has disciplined himself by lifelong training to the development of extended memory, an extension to cover long stretches of the historical past.

For *your* information it can be said that he had an important job to finish, not fully completed when called down into incarnation. Consequently, a good deal of him stayed behind to finish it; and only arrived here in middle life. The same sort of thing is happening now, but in the reverse direction. So you haven't seen as much of me as would otherwise be the case. Just as well perhaps?

G. Trevelyan – see enclosed. The request to 'show a light' came to me from a great and lovely Being who directs the activities of many workers in densest Borderland. This campaign of his is spreading widely 'over there' and no doubt he can start a similar chain reaction 'over here'.

Perhaps a suitable successor to the 'Silent Minute' observance, using light instead of sound. We shall see.

10.7.64

Memo

An emergency meeting of the College of Heralds was held late last night lasting until our dawn. The College is set on the side of a hill, surrounded by woods, gardens, springs, and beside an observatory. It is situated spheres higher than the Borderland region and I ride up to it on my favourite steed. He has learned to accommodate his rhythms to the change required in passing from one sphere to the next.

I did manage to buttonhole the Senior Collegiate to discuss your query. However it soon emerged that I am not allowed to divulge current business. I had to leave before the Conference was over to keep an appointment elsewhere with the Elder Brother who is in charge of the many Groups of missionary volunteers working in lower Borderland's densest jungles on dangerous salvage operations. Dante's description of Hades pales before what is to be encountered in these age-old swamps, black bogs and quicksands. Souls once human, whose identity is almost lost; deliberate followers of the dark road, distracted wandering beings, many creatures sub-human and animal – all these are to be met with, and struggled with and salvaged if at all possible. Although one ventures into these regions clothed in a kind of protective luminous 'asbestos' one emerges shaken and deeply depressed.

The Campaign now launched to Show a Light* was, my good

---

* The reference is to the inauguration, at TP's request, of a campaign known as The Lamp Lighters. Sir George Trevelyan lit the first lamp at Attingham Park.

friend tells me, undertaken on direct instructions from Hierarchical levels. Until these terrible regions have been thoroughly spring-cleaned, gross materialism will continue to infect human consciousness; it is as part of this campaign that we on earth are now asked to show and tend a permanent light at every centre and in every home where the will to good and service is the watchword; and vitally important is the *intent* behind the first lighting of these lamps.

These innumerable spots of flame can become focal points for our aspirations, blending with the lights on etheric levels and beyond. Missionaries will carry the concentrated illumination down into the dark spheres; how can we refuse to respond to the call now reaching us?

12.7.64

What insatiable curiosity Alexias shows about all sort of funny things! Such as who WTP really is and why he rides a horse in Borderland instead of using his wings! A tome of a thousand pages and more would be needed to satisfy this alert and probing intellect, and meanwhile our little book would perish in the deluge. The College of Heralds? Well this is a very ancient body indeed. At present there are seventy-seven members of whom seven are senior Initiates. These seven are now exercising their functions as Heralds and Preparers of the Way – for the third time. In their case the two previous bouts of duty, each lasting about a century of our time, were preludes to the arrival of the Lord Buddha and the Lord Jesus on earth. For the other seventy the present is the first occasion they have been seconded for special duties in this way, on the authority of the planetary Hierarchy.

I don't know them all really well, although I am an attendant member of their College. One of them however is a great friend of mine, a companion through many centuries. He it was who inspired my soldier friend to seek the gift of a daily minute of prayer and silence, a few hours before he lost his earthly life in Palestine in December 1917. The territory, speaking mundanely, where he is active comprises the Near and Middle East, most parts of Europe and the whole of the British Isles. For Britain he has the full co-operation of two of his fellow Heralds, who make up an important Triad. Of course they were behind the purchase of Chalice Well (for their own ends). And now they are behind the Lamp Lighters as a sequel and supplement to the Silent Minute.

The choice of Attingham Park as a launching site for this sequel was owing to its position more or less in the centre of England, from which radiations will extend in every direction like the spokes of a wheel.

But the Gods forbid that WTP should be expected to run still one more campaign. Let's see how much of this chore can be shifted on to G.T's shoulders.

Yes of course I know what your curiosity is after now. 'Preparers of the Way' – for what? For Whom?

There must be a good reason why one is forbidden to answer these questions concretely, why the Spirit must move like a thief in the night of Man's despair. Many of us know that a powerful leaven is now at work, affecting the mental and emotional structures of all forms of life on this planet. Hence our frustration, restlessness, upheavals of every kind, to be seen collectively everywhere as well as in the minds and hearts of individuals. We are at a turning point in human affairs, a terrifying cleansing operation. Yes, you ask, but what next?

This largely depends upon the success or failure of the leavening process, but there could be a swift upliftment within the human mind followed by the advent towards earth levels, and even on earth, of great Messengers from God; and perhaps a Being of the Saviour class. Or if the present effort fails, the arrival of one beside whom Genghis Khan and Hitler would be pygmies. Allow your curiosity to stop at this point so that you can concentrate upon that weaving of the minute area of the tapestry which has fallen to your lot.

Maybe these and similar notes contain material to see the light of day someday, through you. There must be a reason why they are being set down in writing.

Memo

Lazarus (the help or helper of God).
This name was very popular because of its connotations. It is
another Lazarus, an active missionary for Christ's message, who is
referred to in Apocryphal and other writings. It would seem that
the life span allotted to Lazarus of Bethany was due to end some
four years after his revival by Jesus: and so it came about. He was
a worthy but retiring youth, who is said rarely to have left the
home he had with his mother and his sisters; the main object of his
earthly life at this time was to serve as the instrument through
whom Jesus demonstrated the truth that the Last Enemy can be
vanquished. There were at least four such occasions and persons –
a boy, a girl, a young married woman, and Lazarus: news of these
miracles reached me by hearsay.

I never was a member of Jesus' close entourage nor did I follow
in the wake of those who followed. In later life I became a member
of an Order of Mystics who sought Truth within, taking little
interest in the many Messiahs and Prophets of the day. Whilst
deeply impressed and inspired by the goodness, humility and
greatness of Jesus, both as a boy and as a young man, I myself was
never drawn to membership of what then appeared to be just
another new sect of the Jews. The Order to which I came to belong
during the three years of his Ministry enjoined its members to hold
themselves aloof from proselytizing movements of every kind,
secular and religious. It is for this reason that, Joseph of
Arimathea apart and Josephes his son, my contacts with the close
followers of Jesus were few and far between.

21.7.64

I have always been enjoined to preserve my anonymity, whether in
incarnation or not, hence the difficulty about my identity in Jesus'
times. Mine was a patrician family with Assyrian roots and we

revered the gods in the pure uncontaminated Greek sense. Not very sympathetic toward the various contending Jewish sects whose adherents milled round Jesus and the early Nazarenes. One supreme Creator above all gods, yes; but a broad universality of outlook that was as rare in early Christian times as it is today. That is the mental background from which I looked upon Jesus, as a man of the gods and a great seer.

We had estates in Syria and a house near Aleppo: my only brother was an authority on precious stones and metals, and in the first place introduced me to J. of A. who in any case was a friend of my father's. Much to my revered mother's grief I never married and later in life became much withdrawn, working as much *au delà* as on earth, just as I do today. However it is not for WTP to stand between the reader and the message, and I do not think these details are necessary or suitable for the book.

My recent reference to adolescent Nature spirits must have brought you to the conclusion that I am even more daft than you knew me to be. But *all* evolving life grows up from infancy.

30.7.64

Diary of an average night's activities

Schedule to fit a period of five hours' deep sleep in every twenty-four-hour period.
First hour. Arrive at my own home, which is situated in a mountain valley (and on its slopes), two levels of rhythm above the Borderland region which surrounds and (in a way) interpenetrates our own planet. Met by my Arab servitor who prepares the bath (light-colour-music liquid waves) and sets out fresh garments for each visit. Bathe and dress. If time allows, visit my stables and farm, talk to my head gardener about the trees and flowers in the home gardens. Then mount my favourite steed and make the long descending journey into Borderland, to visit the H.Q. offices of the Red Cross Rescue Station (which I have helped to build and

equip, extend and staff, during the past sixty years). Cosmic light cannot reach down to this level. We have therefore our own generators powered by swift streams which cascade down the ravines in the mountains by which the Station is surrounded and protected.

The area of the Station is the equivalent of two square miles on earth. It contains hospitals, rest homes, lecture and concert halls, farms, gardens, children's playgrounds and an animal, bird and insect sanctuary. The Staff quarters alone occupy a site equal to a small garden city on earth, with nearly two thousand occupants – doctors, healers, teachers, nurses, orderlies, musicians, artists: there are rarely fewer than 25,000 persons there including patients, pilgrims, passers-by and missionaries. All the workers are volunteers willing to delay their own evolutionary ascent to more delectable spheres.

The sentinels should not be forgotten. They stand on guard all round the Station circumference, keeping at bay the pressure of waves of darkness by which this area of Borderland is filled almost to overflowing. So strenuous is their work that they have to be relieved at very frequent intervals.

Second hour. Conferences with senior Staff. Discussion of Station problems, tour of inspection, meeting and greeting newcomers, helping to train Staff for special duties; entertaining guests who may visit our Station from other levels of life. And prayer.

Third hour. If there has been a large intake, due to some accident on earth, then my stay is usually prolonged into the third hour. Otherwise I ride round the Station's outer walls and visit the sentinels, and sometimes act as one myself. (A refresher course!)

Fourth hour. Nowadays spent within the College of Heralds, of which I am a member. This is situated on high ground surrounded by lovely groves of trees, planted to provide distant vistas away to the horizons in every direction. The plane itself is three levels of rhythm above Borderland. Listen to and take part in a Conference, conducted usually by a Senior Herald, during which all kinds of problems are discussed and solutions found if possible: for instance, how best to train and equip 'fore-runners', whether to be in bodily incarnation or not; study of the 'temperature' of human consciousness among various tribes, races, nations and individuals on earth; perhaps the equipping of a particular Herald to go forth as Guide to someone on earth who is carrying out a special mission. Above all, intensive training, with 'lamps lit', to be prepared when the supreme Call is sounded.

Usually by now I am watching the clock so to speak, as I dare not overstep the five-hour period allotted to me each night; otherwise bodily life and work in daytime would suffer.

Fifth hour. Unless called away for meetings on higher levels I return to my own home, stable my steed; go into my library (to which a first class observatory is attached) and try to get a little rest. But not for long, because always there is a queue of people waiting in the gardens outside, seeking counsel or solace or healing, or merely companionship. Long before the end of the file is reached I have to call a halt; disrobe, take a bath; put on my earth level garments, and prepare to re-enter my mundane frame. (Most reluctantly!)

This summary only touches upon the very fringe of one's other-worldly activities, which vary according to the needs of the hour and the occasion. Now and again, for instance, one is obliged to ride up into much higher spheres than usual, perhaps at the summons of Messengers or their Principals of the Hierarchy. When this happens, apart from short preparations for the journey made within my own home, at least four hours of the allotted span are taken up in this way. Incidentally, I have built on my estate a very comfortable and inspiring guest house, where friends and colleagues are always welcome, from both sides of the Veil. I only wish I could devote more time to their entertainment.

2.8.64

Devenish. I had a look at it. At present a heavy etheric cloud hangs over the Island. Unless this can be dispersed it will be necessary to select another of the islets in the Lough as the future link between Iona and Avalon.

Last night I took time off to wander round one of the spheres where the pre-natal crèches are housed. So far I have not been able to locate the grandchild* who is to grace your august line before the month is out. I will try again, when I can.

4.8.64

What a funny question to ask! I was 'in the flesh' during those terrible days and weeks, in the W.O., in the H. of C. corridors, in the Lords' smoking room, in the flat of a prominent Minister's mistress and never out of SW1. I was bombed out four times, and bombed *at* over ten times.

Out of the flesh, of course I was at Dunkirk and thereabouts. I did my job, but not as well as it should have been done. (Some success with elementals, winds, weather and currents: but too many alas were drowned.) A much bigger job was helping to stop invasion.

5.8.64

Memo

Walburga Paget pulled the strings for WTP (up to the Cabinet) before the first World War. Lady Isobel Margesson did the same for him before and during the first part of the second. David M. at the time was Chief Government Whip (later Min. of War for a few months). And so, stage by stage, WTP's murky past is being revealed to you!

(When in Constantinople in 1908 I realized that it was already too late to avert the first war. I came home and built a factory at Bristol to make army ration biscuits. Very useful until it met its end by fire late in 1916.)

* Kate, my fourth grandchild.

Wellesley Tudor Pole. Who was the man known to his friends as TP? In one letter he writes: 'I am only a visitor to this particular planet — not one of its regular denizens. I come and go when commanded to do so . . . . I am a modest and anonymous ambassador from elsewhere.'

The Chalice Cup. The 'Cup of Peace'. A shallow blue sapphire bowl, made from crystalline substance and containing floral milleflori designs in blue, green and amber. The flower pattern is interlined by silver-leaf foil of perfect lustre. First discovered under unusual circumstances in 1906 at St. Bride's Well, Glastonbury.

Chalice Well, Glastonbury. Many remarkable acts of healing have been carried out at this blessed spot.

Rayner Johnson's *The Light and the Gate*. In my view the 'Pratt' section of this book is the most balanced and interesting. But why do both Pratt and the Venerable S. rejoice in the assurance that they need not and will not return to earth? I question their authority for this belief. Should not their experience be placed at the disposal of less advanced mortals? What matter if one's own 'salvation' be delayed a few thousand years if meanwhile one can help others along the pilgrim path?

11.8.64

Churchill has always feared the supernatural, not because he thought of it as bunk but because he believed in it. I once heard him remark that tobacco smoke and brandy 'kept his ghosts at bay'. When I warned him that the H. of C. was being tapped during secret sessions, and *proved* it; adding that unless the requisite steps were taken this would continue to the end of the war, unless the Chamber were destroyed meanwhile; 'Uncanny' was all he said, and nothing was done. So, much of Lord Haw Haw's insidious ammunition came to him this way.

Why tell you these things? No one else knows them, but David Margesson may guess a little.

Yes, Walburga was a darling. Right out of the eighteenth century. Autocratic, imperious, witty, warm hearted. Tolerant. Clever. A great lover of animals and birds. A supremely adroit puller of strings in high places. Yet she could not manage her Elizabethan son-in-law and never really forgave him for censoring her Memoirs, which I induced Sir G. Hutchinson to publish. And it was *I* who got the blame from the latter, because he had already put down £500 royalties 'for the spice'.

Perhaps I am suffering from a guilt complex in feeling that I should entertain you with gossip of this kind? That otherwise my influence in your life is too solemn and uplifting???

The Tor dig has started in a blaze of TV and Press publicity. Crowds and much milling. Nothing sensational has yet emerged.

Had I not overheard it myself the following would be too good to be true. A very great lady who shall be nameless, was visited by her guide soon after her passing and offered help and companionship. She replied, 'Well, I am getting along all right, but I *do* miss the company of men *as such.*'

The Tor dig. What is the history of our lovely young man?* Over six foot, vigorous, robust and (no doubt) good looking. Buried carefully in a rock-hewn grave. Someone had cleaved his thigh bone. How and why did he meet his end? Defending a hidden holy relic? Slain in battle somewhere else and brought to the sanctified Tor for burial? He was not a monk I am sure. Or have we dated his bones wrongly, could he have been the victim of ritual murder? A sacrifice of youth and virility to ensure a bounteous harvest? Such ritual murders are still prevalent in some parts of darkest Africa, though nowadays a male child under seven is usually the victim. Shall I have to investigate all this?

Why not look into it yourself? You knew him *very* intimately. And so I think it's your pigeon. Sharpen your psychic wits!

Over thirty years ago I was stopped from continuing to act as a post office between individuals living at different levels of consciousness. The demands absorbed me night and day. Since then I

* During this 1964 Tor dig, a rock-hewn grave containing the bones of a young man was uncovered.

have not been allowed to work along those lines, but rather to try to help people to become their own transmitters and receivers, gradually replacing their yearning for communication by the far more satisfying and permanent method of wordless communion. So many ask me to break my rule, but I dare not admit the thin edge of the wedge.

My little genie has proved his use once more. Bless him! I left the only pen with which I can write, in a post office, and when I returned to search, it had gone. Late the same night it dropped on to my bedside table, *here* and is quite intact.

He does not know how to explain to me the mechanics of the operation. Perhaps as well? In the wrong hands such goings-on could lead to robbery and worse.

5.9.64

Stocktaking

Has the time come when I should take an honest and objective look at where I stand, and what I believe?

If so, and firstly, have I now evolved a personal religion for myself and am I practising it? Or is my conduct solely conditioned by a more or less vague moral code?

Do I really believe in the value of prayer? What do I mean by prayer? Are my prayers affirmative, meditative, petitionary or all three?

Do I *really* believe that the power of the Spirit can be invoked to bring me health, serenity, enlightenment and the capacity to be of service to others? If I do, to what extent am I putting my belief into practice?

What is my life's objective? Have I one? Or do I drift? Are my thoughts and actions, and especially on matters spiritual, influenced by the views and comments of my friends? Or even swayed by a sense of futility or fatality?

In answering these questions for yourself and *to* yourself, complete objectivity should leave no room for self-deception.

107

I am aghast to find that it is a set Evangelical service at which I am expected to speak (or preach?) on Devenish Isle, with the usual trimmings. I thought it was to be an informal gathering just to mark the Saint's anniversary? Whatever one may say someone will take offence, owing to the extreme bitterness still raging over there between Caths and Prots.

Am delighted that what you are now writing is 'writing itself';* and so long as WTP is fully denigrated in it all will be well.

I have the impression that if you are to descend into the realms of notoriety you would prefer to share that experience with a more romantic companion than WTP. Lucifer, for instance? Well! I am on good terms with him, as you know; indeed I am one of his few real friends on this planet. Therefore I could arrange to transfer Your Majesty to his (more or less) safe escort should you so desire.

Here is the Roma Lister book. I made her promise to leave me out of her reminiscences, which she did, apart from an indiscretion connected with the Colosseum – very naughty of her. Whilst babbling on about the doings of society, here and there she comes out with a fragment of occult knowledge of the kind that should have remained secret. Lived in Rome mostly. She was a buddy of mine, and a friend of Walburga's.

How *hard* I try to keep you amused; but can I ever expect to keep you out of mischief?

I don't feel happy at the prospect of a Buda Pest visit for you just now. The stars are not very propitious for this. Lucifer? Yes, one

* *The Swan in the Evening*, Wm. Collins.

day you shall know more. WTP is *not* on his staff, but now and then acts as an intermediary.

I agree with you: the majority of spiritualist services show a touching enthusiasm and simple devotion. After all it is a real solace to many folk to know (through supernatural means) where Grannie really did hide her cameo brooch and how to relieve Aunt Jemima's rheumatism. I do not underrate the value of much that comes through in these ways.

But what one seeks in vain, among all these countless communications, is evidence that the communicators know more than we do, in a spiritual sense? Most of them seem to live in a closed room little larger than they occupied on earth. For instance has anyone from *au delà* ever told you that the lower regions of Borderland cannot be reached effectively 'from above'; so that we on earth must light the beacons for those living in deep darkness there? Don't they *know* this?

19.9.64

A main object for the Lamp Lighter campaign is to establish a safe link or channel between three- and four-dimensional levels of consciousness. A beacon is lit at each end of this channel and the light intermingles within it, giving protection from irresponsible intelligences and from lower astral vermin. Communion and inspiration are thereby safeguarded, and error and irrelevance avoided. It's a step away from automatism and therefore a step UP.

You will soon perceive the truth of this when your own light has been kindled and cherished with the right intent. It is all part of the plan to limit entry into mortal consciousness on the part of astral residues, uncontrolled entities, which now find their way in by the doorways of trance and automatism.

The inflow of the Christ spirit is a personal and unique experience, one which needs to use the purest and safest channels possible and from *within* each one of us.

109

I hope this will reach you before you leave for Paris and Buda. And that all goes well, and that the autumn weather is delightful.

Our blue sapphire bowl once resided at Avignon, probably in Papal times. But not for very long. You may well pick up some of your own past experiences and make one or even two new contacts. I am doing all possible and allowable for the success of your gathering and that you may be safeguarded.

16.10.64

Welcome home! Not too exhausted I hope? An invisible link was forged; but its external counterpart may not have been recognized.

George Trevelyan sounds thrilled with the Jesus glimpses, but apparently not clear about the relevance of the Introduction. However I await his considered comments. I read extracts from the scripts last night to the Senior Staff of our Red Cross Station (translated into Astra Lingua). The interest aroused was profound and exciting. Echoes spread widely.

I gather that the 'Teacher of Righteousness' was a title used by at least three successive Leaders of the Dead Sea sects. This will take some disentangling.

The Labour victory will have knocked a couple of thousands off my meagre savings: so I must tighten my belt.

Give me a call on Monday.

25.10.64

George Trevelyan has been out on his own crusade to explain the significance of the Lamp Lighters' campaign.

The subtlest form of 'matter' perceptible to human sense is the light man produces from gas, oil, coal and magnetic friction. Our planet has to be 'lifted up' (by evolution) into a condition that will make it a more suitable residence for three-dimensional life. In 'lifting up' man-made light with specific intent, we are helping forward the redemption of all matter. This will be too metaphysical for most: hence the campaign is based on simpler theses. And is spreading widely.

26.10.64

During the past weekend I have been doing my best to clear up, and to my satisfaction, certain points concerning the Jesus scripts.

An Authority beyond dispute by me makes it clear that Jesus *was* born in the usual human way; and that his two angelic guardians (who never left him) were present at his conception, having arranged the exact time, day and place beforehand. He was the eldest of Mary and Joseph's family (by three years and nine months): and in the family in due course were two brothers, two foster brothers, and two sisters, one of whom died young.

Now this information is not the fruit of my memory. I never visited his home. It has been 'told' to me in these latter days, and therefore is not first-hand. I was neither a Jew nor a follower of Jesus, I would meet him and see him at the home of his uncle Joseph of Arimathea whenever my affairs took me that way.

7.11.64

In my youth I gave up trying to improve myself. Far more important is how can I serve others from the place where I now stand. There are millions of years available for personal evolution and the less we try to perfect ourselves by self-conscious means the

111

better progress are we likely to make. Somehow one has to learn how to cease being important to *oneself*!

On Mrs. C's query about who believes in reincarnation and where it is taught, any good book dealing with comparative religion will enlighten her. I don't plug any particular truth or thesis. If religions were non-existent this would not affect my personal beliefs based on my own experiences and for which no external props are necessary. And as to the 'glimpses', let those who cannot accept that memory can be exercised in this way, fall back on the value of allegory.

I look forward to other happy meetings with Sally, looking so gay, alive and beautiful on her white pony. I was on the wild moors when we met.

30.11.64

The aura of the coming Messenger has begun to penetrate our human atmosphere. This does not necessarily entail his imminent appearance outwardly. But it is a presage. Before the first great Buddha made his earthly appearance his aura had preceded him by nearly twenty-five years of our time. And Jesus' by nearly half a century! However, 'time' is elastic and on the other hand can become condensed.

3.12.64

Shalom Dom! We should remember that as each Round of evolution reaches the halfway point prior to the upward swing, for which immense effort is needed to create the impetus, two things happen: (1) The arrival within human consciousness of fresh leaven, usually heralding a Messenger or great Teacher (and

112

usually with lesser lights of his own choosing around him). (2) A speed-up in the cleansing karmic process, both for nations and individuals. Quite unpleasant! A kind of Day of Judgement, one that does not require the shedding of our mortal coils but takes place here and *now*.

No wonder if we who carry some of the general karmic burden as well as our own, seem at times to be near breaking point. Yet we should aspire to the carrying of more than what we imagine to be our 'fair share'.

Each Round lasts approximately 25,000 years and we are halfway through the present Round. There are twelve Ages within this period, each lasting about 2,000 years. We are now leaving the Piscean and passing into the Aquarian Age in the House of the Zodiac. When we move house on earth, what commotion! How much more so when all life on our planet begins to trek from one 'house' to another.

The roughly sketched background given above forms the basis of my current life and work. And my freewill within this framework is conditioned by the wishes and requirements of more than one Elder Brother of the Race. One does not publicize these things.

Douglas Fawcett. I only knew him through correspondence about his brothers, whom I did know. However I was partly responsible for getting his publications financed. As you say his remarkable writings will come into their own some day.

10.12.64

I am just posting off my annual donation for the upkeep of a cultured and intelligent woman who has been in a French asylum for years: following a long period of automatism undertaken from the best of motives. But one should not argue from the general to the particular, however terrible the particular can be.

'Death' has only one recognized meaning, namely the destruction or extinction of life. As life cannot be extinguished we speak a falsehood whenever we refer to a person's death.

113

Two people, known to us both, have just crossed the River; Edith Sitwell and Lord Marks. Neither ready for the crossing (to human observation). But then, who is?

I agree that Geraldine Cummins has produced a great deal of very real value. What is absent is discrimination. She will live on through her best work, as should be the case with us all.

Glad you have some sunshine and so are enabled to swim in the Channel comfortably. Don't feel in the least obliged to become an objective Lamplighter. Let your inner lamp shine forth clearly and I will let you off!

16.12.64

I was in London all day yesterday so only received yours from Little Eden* last last night, but none the less welcome for that.

The Quest. Much contained in those automatic scripts† is accurate both in substance and in historic detail. Some of it descended into astralitis without this being apparent at the time to those concerned. Four times my own bodily life was placed in pawn and there is no doubt that the Guardians of those precious Records are unwilling to let them go, and that we have not yet earned the right to use the key which could release them. I expect I (for one) have learnt more of value from this tragic and humiliating failure than from any success I may have had in other ways. If there is to be a sequel this century the right way will be shown and marching orders given. Patience!

As to the mission of the Avalon 'Cup'. That too will be manifest in its own time and way. I hate mystery, but in this instance I have not been given the necessary power to elucidate it.

'Death.' I appreciate and respect all you say and I have explained myself badly. All I am really concerned about is that the word as meaning final extinction should gradually be eradicated from human consciousness. If used, the manner of its use should be qualified. 'Death must die', and it is up to us to hasten the funeral.

* The name of my small house in the Isle of Wight.
† A copy of these scripts, given to me by TP, is in safe keeping.

Up to about 1930 I often acted as a sort of Post Office, indeed a postman, between the levels of consciousness. Suddenly I was stopped in my tracks, resulting in much misunderstanding among very many sorrowing souls – and very real grief to myself at the sight of such distress. Until I realized that the immense joy of *communion* once achieved far outweighed the merely *temporary* satisfaction of communication by words.

So few can appreciate this; it is natural to want to devise an immediate way through by 'telephone'; to hear the beloved voice once more, to bring back the conditions and the methods we use between us when both are in the flesh and subservient to its five senses. You and Sally will come nearer and nearer together *in full reality* as use of intermediaries is given up. Nearer I mean in realization and understanding, in feeling and happiness and love.

On Sunday last my phone scarcely once stopped ringing, much to the disgust of Kippy, my Corgi. Finally he lost patience, hurled himself on the flex and bit it through: with the result that the ringing stopped and the phone went dead. Then with a smirk of satisfaction Kippy lay down to sleep the sleep of the just.

Have been destroying tons of scripts and writings that have been accumulating over the century. Simply no way of storing them. In one way or another our effort to bring Jesus out of the fog of ecclesiasticism and misinterpretation will succeed. No matter if in the process incredulity and criticism are provoked, *he* will grant us his blessing and recompense. Whatever else may have proved worth while or not, *1964* will NOT have been wasted and we have done the best we could.

Yes, I know how fanatical I sound about the use of the word 'death'. I simply obey instructions to try to eradicate from the hearts and minds of men all sense of extinction. As this is done, an immense dark cloud will lift.

Jesus' outcry on the Cross
That portion of the Christos principle which had individualized
within the aura of Jesus, and which in fact permeated his mind and
body, could not be subjected to the experience of crucifixion. Had
it remained with Jesus, no crucifixion could have taken place, a
miracle of release would have happened.

As the overshadowing began to withdraw, from individuality to
principle, the sense of loneliness (and even of failure) brought
forth that cry of agony and desolation. Perhaps if and when the
time comes to write a biography, this may receive a measure of
comprehension, but I feel it would be premature to include it in
our present book? I daresay Steiner has written about this.
Post-mortem evolution. In my view evolution never ceases except
when man temporarily becomes involved in a period of devolu-
tion. There is no such thing *anywhere* as an absolutely static
condition. You have watched Sally's growth and development
since her departure: surely this demonstrates the point to your
satisfaction? Elsewhere in J.S's book it is said or implied that only
when the soul has been 'purified' (is not that progress?) is it ready
to reincarnate. If this be true why do so many new born babies
show signs of depravity, or anyway indications far removed from
'purity of soul'? Am I showing prejudice against 'communications'
of this kind? In his *New Humanity Now* M.G. asserts that God's
Majesty and greatness only come out most fully when He is
suffering, inferring that the same is true for man. The value
sadistically placed on pain, the grotesque speculations and
immature conceptions of the functions and qualities of the Deity,
are enough to make one despair of theology.

As you know WTP was not a follower of Jesus in the exact sense.
He was, as now, a Universalist, belonging (then as now) to the
Schools of the Mysteries, or rather those engaged in research into

the secret laws of nature. *Not* for use in magic, nor for personal ends, but to be in a better position to serve Life in all its forms. Whilst conversant with the tenets of the world's philosophies and religions, he and his fellow students identified themselves with none: study of *all* systems was, and is, our field. Hence the interest in the Essenes, and the various revolutionary groups of that time and place (Palestine and the Near East), which included the teaching of Jesus (towards which I was immensely attracted). Our training was severe, life-long, and remains age-long.

There is a stringent rule: never to speak from the standpoint of personal authority. One may outline what one experiences, or thinks, or witnesses *first hand*, one may even express opinions and personal beliefs. But one may never set up as a Teacher whose word is Law.

Now WTP was not present at Calvary. He is no authority on what took place there. So far as he is aware, no one actually present in the flesh was capable of seeing anything deeper than the material events themselves; so he has not even so much as hearsay evidence for the statements made by him about these stupendous happenings. His information comes from a Source that cannot even be named. That he himself regards the wisdom and authority of this Source as beyond question is beside the point – he is only allowed to speak of such things as if he offered opinion merely, or speculation as to what may well have been the case.

Whilst at times I *do* seem to speak as if with authority, especially when describing what I saw or experienced first hand, I never intend my words to imply final and authoritative pronouncements on Truth as if I were beyond the liability to error or illusion. I put forward what I believe to be a correct explanation of the facts, but I claim no authority whatever for the validity of my beliefs and have no wish to propagate them. It is without egotism and in all humility that I share my experience and my reflections with my fellows.

26.1.65

Yesterday I went to *The Times* to disclose material and information which W.C. had asked me to withhold until he had left us.

117

No one will ever know of the W.C./WTP war relations. Curious how great ones after they go hence seek rest in quite humble activities, which call for no great mental strain and bring relief. When Queen Victoria was asked what she wished to do, she opted for running a draper's shop where she herself could do the buying and control the staff and set the fashions. (Which kept her happy for a long time.) Apparently this idea had lodged in her sub-conscious during most of her last life on earth. Pope John is now enjoying the life of a simple village priest. I once came across Brunel, carving models of bridges and trains and taking them round to entertain children. I should not be surprised if Einstein is not a simple Maths master at an elementary school. Churchill may well decide to run a tobacco shop with an Off Licence for beer and spirits. You see such people are not ready at once to undertake spiritual tasks, yet they feel the need for action in ways that are not too demanding.

The *British Weekly* has come out with an article suggesting that a new form of Christianity may be on the way, outside the orbit of the Churches.

And so we plod along our humble ways, often quite unaware why and how we are being used. Strange* that Lawrence, as reported in automatic communications, seems to have no concern for his fellows but to be wrapped up in hopes of his own salvation. *That* only comes when we cease to seek it and learn the need of anyway a modicum of selflessness.

3.2.65

Almost certainly *A Man Seen Afar* will call for some kind of sequel, biography or otherwise. And so, place your guns at the standby meanwhile.

I was in the Lebanon at the time of the Crucifixion, looking after my father's farm, which included a *lovely* grove of cedars. I was not directly involved as you know; indeed had I been one of Jesus' followers I could not have recounted what I have, *objectively*.

The fact that Aramaic contains no imperatives, which only

* Not strange, in my opinion!

appeared in Greek and Latin translations, raises important issues. Perhaps Jesus spoke to Satan in some archaic and occult tongue? Otherwise it would have to be something like: 'Thy place is in the shadows behind me.'

What a pity the Gospels give no first hand narratives! Polycarp's diary from St. John's dictation on Patmos, lying buried beneath the House of Justinian in old Stamboul, would reveal much truth as to facts.

On an authority far nearer first hand than the N.T. writers, I am satisfied that Jesus made his last dispositions regarding his mother etc., whilst still in prison. Far too important to wait for this until his body was dying on the Cross. Also when murderers, brigands and thieves were being crucified it was the Roman custom to keep a space some fifty yards clear all round the place of execution. Last-minute rescues were often attempted by friends of bandits etc. A precaution certainly not relaxed for Jesus, even though the cowardice of his immediate followers reduced any such risk from that quarter: but the common people were inflamed and revolution was in the air, so precautions would have been doubled. The only people within earshot of Jesus on the Cross would have been the Roman soldiers and their officer, and a legal procurator from the Roman Law Courts, present to register the due carrying out of the sentence (similar in some ways to our Coroner). Apart from these there may have been one or two representatives of the Sanhedrin, granted special permits for the occasion. The three Marys and others would have been beyond earshot and so if any messages were received for them at that time they must have been conveyed later by permission of the Roman officer in charge of the proceedings.

Who therefore was likely to have recorded any words of Jesus? The Procurator perhaps? The soldiers were illiterate.

17.2.65

I am a little concerned that I throw no light in our book on Jesus' brothers and sisters, whom I never met but vaguely remember seeing at a distance. Two of the brothers were I believe adopted

119

and not his blood relations. The two sisters I think died young, anyway have left no impression. What became of the brothers and why do they never enter closely into Gospel narratives? Jesus always seemed so solitary amongst his family and so much closer to Joseph of A. and Josephes. Why this blank in my glimpses? Will it ever be filled?

My own family had few close Jewish friends and were what today would be called landed gentry, with inherited means and property: town house near Jerusalem, estates in the Lebanon, *pied-à-terres* near both Alexandria and Rome. We travelled widely and were patrons of the Arts, students of Greek and Egyptian philosophies, archaeologists too. The Roman occupation of Palestine, Syria etc., did not affect our way of life, in fact we had many friends among the Roman aristocracy. Revolutions came and went but we were not involved. With such a background, an 'Internationalist' in outlook, a follower of no set religion, it is natural that I was brought up with no Jewish ties; and so my contacts with Jesus could be regarded as casual, and I never visited his home; whilst, as you know, I was in the Lebanon at the time of his crucifixion. Hence the objectivity of my glimpses and their fragmentary character.

One cannot recover memories all in one go, it is a gradual process. In my present incarnation I was born into the middle class with immediate forebears West of England freehold farmers. Without being snobbish (I hope!) this has never seemed to fit with either my Tudor background or my earlier lives. Although I *was* born a slave in Egypt once, as you know from *The Silent Road* (and for a special reason). I can hear you saying 'Stop all this babble and tell me about my own background.' Fair enough. However I believe Sally hopes to work out a kind of genealogy for you, from which I may crib in due course.

A month ago I found myself needing a piece of medieval amber from the Near East, in connexion with a particular item of research (I mean by medieval the setting, not of course the age of the amber itself). Abdul Baha gave me a fine amber rosary in 1922, about the time he gave me his camel hair cloak; greatly valued ever since, but not medieval in setting. I mentioned my need to my little genie, a few days ago, but not with really serious intent. Today arrived from Kansas City of all places, and from a

120

complete stranger, a lovely amber rosary of the period I needed. The note with it from a Mrs. M. M. Parkinson said, 'When recently in Palestine I came across the rosary I now enclose. I feel that its original owner would like you to have it.' (No mention of who the original owner was, if she knew!) Very alarming these incidents. far too reminiscent of Aladdin's Wonderful Lamp for my liking. But isn't it the time element in this case which is so intriguing?

24.2.65

The danger of misunderstanding arising when short answers are given to questions about metaphysics, makes me chary in dealing with them so. However: each group soul possesses its own Guardian or Elder Brother, who is available for consultation even after one is no longer part of a group soul. But this does not mean he is a *personal* Guide. Spiritualists use the word far too loosely; 'Your Guide asks me to tell you this or that', can give a wrong impression. Help or guidance is of course always available to those who seek it prayerfully and humbly, but one's evolution has to go a *very* long way before affinity attracts a personal Guide in the sense of an alter ego, who so to speak is one's own property and remains so as one travels across Eternity.

At last I have ferreted out of Berlin a copy (in English) of Paul Winter's *On the Trial of Jesus.* A very important book, by an erudite German Jew, who lost all his close relatives in the pogroms and whose great scholarship is therefore somewhat biased by personal bitterness. He shows very clearly that Jesus could not possibly have met his end on the morning after his arrest, and indeed from quite different source material his conclusions on this and some other crucial points agree with mine. I cannot think why this book is not more read over here. No serious student can afford not to read it.

Here is a draft copy of Spearman's contract. The terms are about as usual, but I shall have minor alterations to make. My solicitors will vet the terms for us and advise on the formation of a simple Trust to hold the copyright on your and my behalf.

We shall be able to refund ourselves for preliminary expenses, typing, postage etc., from our Trust funds, including that of forming the Trust itself. We shall then be free to allot the Trust's income as and when we wish to charities or to other philanthropic ends; but I hope you and I will agree that the Chalice Well Trust should be the principal beneficiary; whilst the terms should allow us room to manoeuvre in deciding our charitable policies?

Meanwhile we can agree the terms of the contract in principle, after scrutiny, but it will be made between the publishers and our own Trust so soon as this is formed.

Delighted that the sun shines so warmly, I hope and believe, for your sojourn in Guernsey.

We used to spend summer holidays there, whilst I was in my early teens. Once while there, when I was fourteen or so, an autocratic old aunt by adoption cabled for me to be sent to Venice. She lived in what seemed to me then to be the height of grandeur, on two immense floors of a crumbling and far from watertight palace on the Grand Canal, with three uniformed domestics of great age, and a kind of Major Domo. The place seemed always full of chattering elderly ladies, eternally flapping their wings which consisted of diaphanous draperies, shawls, silk shoulder spreads, capes of all sizes and shapes. . . . Apart from all this, I seem to remember a continual conflict of interest and influence between masses and masses of cut flowers and shocking smells arising from the canal. One day I was taken to call on Eleonora Duse, who conducted me around her exquisite walled garden and presented me with 'a red rose for England'. Except for Sarah Bernhardt, whom I was only near once (bowing distance), Duse seemed to my young soul to be the embodiment of all the tragedies capable of being experienced by man.

Do not take it that WTP's method of flitting in and out of incarnation (by stages so to speak) is common experience. It just happens that the jobs he does make for a certain mobility and even freedom from the 'Wheel'. But this does not indicate that he is an advanced soul or separate from the madding crowd.

23.3.65

Yes I have that booklet. Much of it is pure astralitis. The Abbey site was bogland when Joseph of Arimathea settled with his followers around the Chalice spring. It was nearly two and a half centuries later that the first rather primitive buildings were erected where the Abbey ruins now are, and in due course these contained a Chapel to Our Lady and another one dedicated to J. of A. Everything except the below-ground foundations was swept away by fire (possibly twice), and finally about eight hundred years ago the Abbey began to be built; and extended to become the wealthiest ecclesiastical estate in England, with Abbots more interested in political power and prestige and material affluence than in their religious responsibilities. And so the plum was ripe for Henry's plucking, and the Abbey's downfall resounded through the land.

Jesus never came to Avalon in the flesh but he did accompany J. of A. once or twice in his thought-body, when a boy and later as a young man. Archangels don't appear personally in the manner described and carry on conversation in human style with human persons. They operate in an entirely different way (too long to go into here).

Lough Erne. When I visited Devenish and other Isles on Lough E. about half a century ago, the negative forces there were shrouded in a blanket of sleep. It was clear to me then that these centres would never be spiritually active again until the negative influences had been aroused and by chemicalization converted for positive and evolutionary purposes. Before the Christian era and on occasions since, the natural telluric and astral currents connected with the Lough have been utilized negatively by certain Intelligences of the Left Path, and various black magical processes have been employed in the attempt to destroy the true spiritual quality of the Islands' atmosphere. Similar conditions have pervaded the Tor Hill at Glastonbury, where we have been engaged in speeding up the chemicalization process, thereby releasing the negative vibrations set up long ago by human agency; and such processes are going on now all over the planet, causing all the turmoil and apparent disaster through which we are living at the end of an Age, and all in accord with Biblical prophecy. By conversion of these freed forces the Energies of the Light are preparing the way for a new and better chapter in human history.

These important processes are normally under the supervision of our Elder Brothers, but on occasion releases take place before the right conditions have been prepared for dealing with them. Something of the sort seems to have been going on around the Lough Erne centres. Energies in themselves are neither good nor bad, they are available for use positively or negatively and can affect us accordingly. In the negative aspect they may prove unpleasant. But 'evil' must never be personalized.

3.4.65

April has bowed himself in with geniality. Or is April a She? In any case let us give thanks.

From time to time we give concerts and readings in the central domed hall of the Rescue or Red Cross Station with which I have been associated since its inception at the beginning of this century. Quite recently most of our book was read out to an attentive audience of Station dwellers, convalescing after the shock (to them) of unexpected transition from earth. I was highly amused afterwards to overhear a conversation between two dear old fogies, recent arrivals, great friends, but somewhat bored at not being ready to go forward yet upon their upward way. Said one to the other: 'Well! What did you make of all that?' The other replied: 'All very strange to me. Has anyone ever before had the audacity to stand up and say, "I was there when it all happened"? It does make me very doubtful, that two thousand years should have passed before such experiences were recorded. Who is he anyway?'

To which the response was as follows. 'You'd better be careful what you say. I believe he's a person of some importance here, so don't get us turned out!'

I heard no more. Yes, I suppose audacity *is* the word! These old dears have not yet even managed to cast aside the facsimile of the earthly form and garments, and so appear to others as well as themselves elderly and somewhat crotchety.

It's only fair to add that many who heard the transmission of the main contents of our book were deeply impressed and absorbed. Two of the senior medical staff, capable of the effort, got leave to go and consult the Akashic Records, for confirmation and elucidation. Wish them luck! Trying to find a rare book in the British Museum Library can take weeks of patience, getting meanwhile every kind of book save the one wanted. But it is a million times more difficult to turn up specific records in the immense Akashic Library! Someone I know has been hunting certain details of the fifth century B.C. for over thirty years of our time!

7.4.65

That rendezvous with Nature sounds alluring although some of these places are run on drastically austere lines. I recall that at Champneys, at the end of my thirty-third day of fasting, the very idea of food had become distasteful to me.

'Weeping Angel' scripts continue to go around. I too cannot bring myself to take these outpourings seriously. All I can say for certain is that whilst conditions favouring a deepening of human perception are being improved now, a special impetus to this process is due before 1967 is over. If meanwhile we are jolted into nuclear war, well, the curtain will not rise but come down. Believe it or not, it seems that our book itself is due to take part in the opening of doors long closed.

The beacon being kindled in Columba's shrine on June 6th will be visible for miles over land and sea and is to be marked on Admiralty charts.

Sally's reference to de Chardin and the possessive walled-in priests 'over there' lusting for converts to the faithful still in prison, reminded me how Pope John waved aside all the ceremonial awaiting him and went off into Retreat in an olive grove. *What* a contrast!

9.4.65

There were no swarms of locusts at the time of Calvary (too early in the year). But a darkening at noon I have myself experienced in the Middle and Near East; sometimes caused by dust or sand-storms, sometimes by a kind of atmospheric fog due to a sudden temperature inversion. A great chilling of the air took place so soon as Calvary began, similar, but not the same exactly, as the chill to be noted when astral doors are opened at a seance. It was this sudden chill which caused a thick mist to obscure the sun and induced darkness and foreboding. But by sunset all was clear.

Glastonbury
16.5.65

The gardens here are full of late spring freshness and fragrance. The inner atmosphere too all of peace, and a strange alluring sense of promise with it. . . .

I met a fellow with whom I was at 'school' some three thousand years ago (a Greek Mystery emporium of a very interesting kind). We meet so very rarely although of approximately the same grade of Initiation. It turns out that he has been on Jesus' H.Q. Staff since the Renaissance, quite a long spell of duty by mortal standards. And now, he tells me, he is seconded to act as A.D.C. to a Forerunner of the Coming One, an equivalent more or less of John the Baptist, one whom I should like to meet before departing hence. Meanwhile, so pleased am I at meeting such an old (but still so youthful!) friend that I at once invited him to stay with me a while. He is a splendid horseman and will revel in those fine steeds which honour my stables with their presence.

All this is very much by the way, but what interests me is the purpose for which my long absent colleague is visiting Chalice Well? He couldn't or wouldn't tell me. I have been guessing and consequently my spirits, depressed by all the tangles and financial problems, have improved.

He had just come from taking an official part in the Wesak ceremonies in that strange far-off Tibetan valley: one that has its own peculiar connexions with Avalon and the vale between the Tor and Chalice Hill. I chaffed him for keeping such exalted company, momentarily forgetting his position on Jesus' personal Staff for so many centuries!

Glastonbury
21.5.65

My colleague of long ago was not in the flesh. He would not be drawn about his mission or details of his new Master, and this in spite of the fact that we are such old and faithful friends. I cannot really understand why it has been so long since we worked closely together, both in bodily form at the same time. I have told him on no account to reincarnate just when I am on the point of discarnating. Someday maybe I will tell you more about this delightful, spirited and courageous character, who I am sure has far outstripped me in the spiritual elevation of his connexions. Bless him, especially if as a result of our renewed contact I may become less of a black sheep.

Weather gorgeous. Moors enchanting. Apple blossom perfect.

26.5.65

Why can't I mean that I have been in disgrace? Am I ever out of it, one way or another? I will think about living dangerously. Although that is what I have always done, there is no general recipe for it that can be shared *safely*.

I heard a tape recording of a talk by Martin Israel and it was very evident he was being talked through, from a fluent and admirable source.

The Cocked Hat Club of the Society of Antiquaries press me to dine with them at the Swan Inn, Wells, on July 2nd. They ask if they may be allowed to inspect what they call my 'sapphire Cup'!

A very strange series of quite un-ordinary events led last week to WTP pulling an ancient clergyman out of a pit of depression wherein he had resided since his demise in 1910! I had to go to the village church where he held sway. And so life moves forward. Or we hope it does!

3.6.65

Longinus. Enclosed cuttings belong to Eddie Campbell and should go back to him in due course. Some of their contents represent purely sensational and therefore unreliable data. I knew the Dr. Stein referred to, who was an erudite historian, but I have no feeling that this particular spear is genuine. Even if it is, its associations have proved pretty horrible.

128

Aleister Crowley once crossed my path and I had to wrench a young and talented undergrad. from out of his clutches. As to the Holy Shroud, no time for detail today, only that whenever I enquire about its authenticity in quarters knowledgeable I am met with evasive replies. I know that Jesus himself intended no *material* relics of his earthly sojourn to remain identifiable.

7.6.65

John 12.v.32. 'And I, if I be lifted up from the earth, will draw all men unto me.'

Whoever quoted this saying interpreted it as referring to the bodily upliftment of Jesus on the Cross. ('This he said signifying what death he should die.') A tragic misinterpretation which no doubt formed the principal basis for the subsequent ecclesiastical doctrine that salvation is solely dependent on the suffering and 'death' of Jesus upon the Cross. ('He died that we might live.') What a disastrous misconception! He spoke not of the literal crucifixion but of the upliftment of his consciousness throughout his earthly life, the emergence from the material to the spiritual, which would have the effect of drawing humanity (and hence all life upon our planet) after him. A process which has not even yet got into its stride.

8.6.65

This infliction in the midst of your hectic two London days is just to thank you for yours of 6th and to wish you every blessing at all your appearances public and private on the Stage of Life.

Beacon Sunday went well on Iona but I have not yet had the details.

How *relieved* WTP is that Alexias does not do this or that, just because WTP seems to imply that she should! In mine of yesterday I did not mean to belittle the symbolic significance of the Crucifixion as a material mode of being 'lifted up', but to indicate that Jesus meant his words to be interpreted in a much wider and fuller sense. A spiritual upliftment upon which he has been engaged for many thousands of years, both here and elsewhere.

13.6.65

Molly Duncan and escort descended upon me yesterday. I suppose she is or has been one of the leading non-professional mediums of the last half-century; now frail bodily but still plucky in mind and spirit. I showed her the Cup, the story of which was unknown to her.

Without trance, this was her comment. 'This vessel is so full of healing power because it was once touched by Jesus. It has been preserved to rise out of the waters in these latter days for a special purpose.' (A reference to its emergence from a well?) 'Do not keep it wrapped up but let it remain exposed in your little sanctuary. This will enable those responsible for its destiny to make their desires known.'

I find messages of this kind very tantalizing!

12.7.65

Welcome Home! beloved voyager. A little rest now is commanded by WTP on celestial advice.

As to the book, nothing sensational has occurred during your absence. I have seen no reviews save one (enclosed). Phone and verbal comments have been many and perhaps one's friends are

130

too polite to express anything but appreciation: really constructive comment has not yet materialized. Sales continue well, and I will get the latest figures in time to include with this. No American bite so far: but a Texas lady of matronly magnificence flew over to see me last weekend and then flew straight back, carrying copies of the book, more orders to follow. Did you show *A.M.S.A.* to any of your brother pen men and was Dubrovnik a real success? Life for me has been so hectic that I could not follow your peregrinations as closely as I had intended. *Mea Culpa!*

Our Chalice Well Copyright Trust is now in being and Michael Crichton has joined our Board, so we shall be a congenial Triad for running the Trust and eventually disposing of its (hoped-for) revenues.

My long weekend at Glastonbury left me exhausted but on the whole satisfied. Word had got round that I was expected; with the result of an influx of those seeking advice etc., from many parts and even abroad. Franz Verkade came over from Holland, a seer in his own right, a C.W. Companion since 1960; he echoed what Inayat Khan said about C. Well as being the holiest centre in Europe and possibly in the whole world, and this was stated with sober conviction. The roses in the C.W. gardens are something quite out of this world, in spite of wind and rain. Strangers to me, met in the gardens, exclaimed, 'this place and its atmosphere are wonderful beyond words.' They really felt so.

At the recent Roselaleham conference in Devon a Dr. Westlake made a violent attack on Sir William Crookes' character and this got into the Press. I am furious at these efforts to smear the reputation of a fine man who was a close friend. He was undoubtedly over-credulous in matters psychic; but sincere, honest, humble and a plucky pioneer. I do what I can to counter this post-mortem vendetta. As you know he reverenced and was keenly interested in what my Cocked Hat Club friends now insist on calling the 'blue sapphire saucer'.

Fourteen of its twenty members were at the lunch at Wells to which I was invited as the guest of honour (very embarrassing for WTP.) Said to be one of the most ancient and exclusive clubs in the world, so much so that its very existence has been unknown to me hitherto. Applicants however suitable do not get the chance of joining whilst the present twenty remain alive. Introductions (as so

131

often) were casual and made *sotto voce*. Among those present were: The principal Curator of the British Museum (Antiquities); the Custodian of the Queen's collection at Windsor Castle; an historian (from Scotland?) who was apparently a Knight Garter of Arms; the Curator of the London Museum (a glass expert); Custodian (or something similar) of the Oxford Museum, with Bodleian connexions; Dr. Ralegh Radford and several high-ups beyond my ken.

The atmosphere was archaeologically esoteric with an admixture of modern erudition and social grace. After lunch the Chairman voiced very modestly the wish of all present to be allowed to examine the Avalon blue sapphire vessel. This was accordingly produced by WTP and handed round the table, being carefully studied by each of the fourteen there assembled. The final and unanimous verdict: 'We have never seen a similar piece. It appears to be unique, and that being so it is not possible to date its origin and age exactly. However, due to the good preservation of this remarkable object we do not think that it can be of ancient manufacture.'

Then came the questions. Where and when found? What was to be its future? What were WTP's views and intentions? Were photos available? Followed by a learned discussion on *millefiori* coloured mosaic glass in general and puzzlement at how the silver foil was inserted in this particular piece.

Now we come to an interesting and unexpected episode. You may remember that three 'maidens' were associated with the finding of this Cup in 1906. My sister Katharine, and Janet and Christine Allen (close friends of hers). Christine married twice later on and as Christine Sandeman was our first Resident Custodian at C.W. (She is now a widow and lives in S. Africa.) Janet never married and later became a R.C. nun and 'died' nearly twenty years ago. K. my younger sister never married, and as you know lives now at Letchworth. Whilst the Cup was being handed round, Janet, wearing convent garb, suddenly appeared to me standing well up over the centre of the table, holding in her hands a replica or etheric counterpart of the vessel. She was smiling and radiant and her garments shimmered with luminosity. After saluting me she turned first to her right and then left and waited . . . and shortly was joined by the other two (K. and C.) and the triad made a circle with hands held; the Cup meanwhile seeming to be suspended in the air in the centre of the circle. Then Janet, speaking to her two companions, said (nodding toward the Cup), 'Evidently our mission still remains to be completed. May Christ and his angels be with us in our task.' The vision then faded, but a kind of radiance continued for a while to linger in the room. An upper room at the Swan Hotel, Wells.

21.7.65

Yes, one misses serious constructive criticism, even if it be hostile. Many readers say they get more and more from repeated reading of the book; but they don't say *what*! Its reception *au delà* is far more discriminating. Many thousands have already had access to it. I have been told that the disquiet to be caused among armour-plated materialists and some egocentrics is a sign to be welcomed. May it be so. I await the mature verdict (on the book's mission) of Those who in fact launched the project and are using it for their own ends. . . .

I think my vision in younger days was less earth-soiled; more innocent, less unquestioning, freer from mundane complexities. Perhaps less deep, and without the didactic note which has crept in since my late maturity. On the other hand, a larger measure of certitude, joy, and even patience, has come to me in later life. *How* you do love asking questions! Are you not tired of my scrawls?

7.8.65

The Tor dig is on and promises well: by 21.8.65 there should be some valuable results for the Companions to see. We now have the area of the foundations of the *original* church demarcated. It is over ninety feet in length and must have been a very imposing edifice: far earlier in date than the sixth-century Abbey down below in the valley, and one of the most important historical and religious sites in England. (The Christ influence is still there.) Has the National Trust enough vision to co-operate in preserving the whole site properly, when we have ended the scrutiny, prepared the plans, filled in and levelled the area and arranged for re-turfing? Try to stir their imagination in regard to their most important property in the U.K.

25.8.65

My dense non-percipience is, I feel sure, well known to you (and perhaps deplored?). But it *was I* who authorized the removal of the modern concrete floor from within the Tor tower. It was necessary to uncover, remove, and re-inter elsewhere all traces of black and grey magical practices from that spot. And to exorcise. I had also asked Sally to come up there after your own departure, and after the exorcism (the latter very exhausting for WTP); with her choir and full musical arrangements, in order to bring back the original Joseph of Arimathea harmonious rhythm to the whole Tor.

I wonder whether Sally via Lady S. (sometimes) would care to secure and pass on comments about Rudolf Steiner's present activities and outlook? He tells me very little, but then the pressure of others who want to tell me about themselves rarely if ever ceases, and so leaves little room for maybe more important activities of this kind.

Many people ask for a copy of the impromptu talk I gave at Chalice Well. What did I say that is worth recording; and can you or someone present summarize it, if such a task is worth the doing?

Drive down quietly and without undue haste. When I was being driven from Glastonbury to Bath yesterday, three separate and contrived accidents were narrowly averted. Other cars had less luck.

Thank you, my very dear, for bringing the fragrance of your presence to my lonely abode.

By now you will have twigged the mission of your missing ring.* Very simple. Its original owner is more interested in you and your destiny than is your own mother. Although the former is a little far off now from mundane realms, her curiosity was aroused by a fresh influence that seemed to have entered your life. She wanted a closer look at what this might be. I wore her ring for an hour and through it she was then able to satisfy her curiosity and even to gain a measure of enlightenment on her own current affairs (yours too).

The Nanteos Bowl. I know its history to some extent and have seen the photographs. Little is now left of it, because so many people have nibbled fragments when seeking healing from it. Scientists date its woodwork to the 10th century A.D., but could be mistaken. Certainly its aura, though now mixed, seems to possess Jesus qualities. Had its destiny been to influence 20th century thought it would *not* now be in a museum. 'By their fruits' etc., and even material objects have certain powers as to their movements: *vide* your ring.

So glad all went well in Wales. You must have passed Unla Water House where my very dear Walburga Paget spent her last years. Yes I used to see Mrs. Osborne Leonard (and Feda) fairly

---

* I left my emerald ring, inherited from my paternal grandmother, in his bathroom when I went to wash my hands. Where now is this beautiful ring? I had no TP or 'little genie' to call upon when it was stolen, along with most of my (few) other valued pieces of jewellery, in London, some years later.

frequently, a lovely person and an immense source of solace to thousands. Latterly she too realized the value of the coming transition from communication to communion, as a needed step forward in human evolution.

Did I tell you of the Jesuit priest from Oxford (a water diviner in his private time) who studied recently the underground sources of Chalice Well, on the spot? Afterwards he expressed amazement at finding that the water feeding the spring is 'already blessed', long before it gushes forth into the Well.

The Tor School will have to close down finally at the end of December. The Chalice Well Trust has first option to purchase, but no means to do so. We are faced by a most critical problem: should the Bank insist on an auction, a brewery may step in (as it tried to do when I bought the property in 1959). We *must* not allow C.W's amenities to be endangered. What to do? My wealthy widow friend would like to help, but I am not going to allow her Trustees to cry out that I am a robber of widows and orphans!

24.9.65

My Bavarian friend Karl writes: 'Immensely grateful for the book (*A.M.S.A.*) which has completely overwhelmed me.'

I have known him since he was a happy youngster, a keen yachtsman, eldest son of landed gentry of wealth and repute. In the last war he was anti-Nazi and suffered cruelly. Then the Russians came, shot his father in front of his mother, who died from the shock. Then they tore Karl away from his wife and two small sons and sent him to the Siberian salt mines for fifteen years, without any charge against him; just because the Russian General wished to take over the castle and estate and all possessions. His wife, an aristocrat, kept going by running a chocolate shop. One card a year came to her from Karl, but censored so that it was indecipherable. Finally he escaped and after a year of agony managed to get back, a wreck, unrecognizable by his children and a burden to his wife. I was able to help him a year or so ago, and

136

fortunately love has persisted and a home has been re-created and life once again becomes possible.

How trivial seem most people's troubles in comparison, even if nature does usually provide an anodyne in the face of tragedy such as this on the grand scale. Anyway here is a case where *A.M.S.A.* has brought a real measure of solace and inspiration. Karl is no purveyor of empty phrases.

2.11.65

Yours full of interest and may the Devon trip prove refreshing and the moor air stimulating. You are right I feel sure about Elizabeth of Austria. Knowing she wished to preserve anonymity I have been careful all these years to respect it. I find her occasionally, kneeling quietly in my little sanctum, sometimes crying, at other times radiant and joyous. I suppose Walburga P. must have spoken to me about her, but my feeling is that they were antipathetic to one another. W. of course was also a great beauty in her time, but Germanic rather than Austrian in type. I find that Servers of a very high order now frequent my sanctum, using it as a kind of *camera obscura* (if that is the right term) for appraising conditions in the human atmosphere on our planet. They bring strong healing influences (as you say) and we should find means for utilizing these, telepathically and otherwise. The sapphire bowl* is of course a unique focus in itself.

9.11.65

When R.C. property is de-consecrated a vaccuum is created and, either with or without official volition, adverse forces enter in: *unless* the necessary steps are taken by experts. There may be no

---

* The bowl remained chiefly in his 'sanctum' during the last years of his life. I often saw it there.

sinister intent behind the de-consecration ritual, but on occasion there is. The Belgian Order of the Sacred Heart sold the C.W. property as a whole in 1909, after it had been empty for a while. Alice Buckton bought it and ruled there for many years. Results were mixed and ultimately the good lady became deranged and eccentric to a degree. She leased the school buildings to two schoolmasters who eventually bought the whole property from her executors, and carried on until I bought it in 1959. I then took what steps I could to free the whole area from previous karma and from adverse vibrations emanating from the Tor, these going back to the days of magic and blood sacrifice. This process will I trust be completed before I pass hence. Meanwhile I am working out certain methods which if the Trustees adopt them (at my expense) will release the healing potential of the Chalice Well spring waters, in a manner suitable to the requirements of the present century.

19.11.65

In 1942 my Lansdowne Road house was gutted, whilst I was in the basement from whence extrication was hazardous. All my old silver, tapestries, Persian rugs and Eastern possessions went up in flames: a collection which had taken half a century to amass. War-time Government Insurance, after a wait of five years, amounted to about 5% of the value. No doubt I was meant to take to heart the unwisdom and the selfishness of laying up treasure on earth; or of loving lovely *things* too much for their own sake. I wonder whether a similar reminder has now fallen to your lot?

Spearmans gave away my home address and now I am beseiged daily by uninvited callers from the U.K., U.S.A. and Europe. And at a time when I am under the weather with 'flu. And my housekeeper distracted by Kipps' strange and unidentifiable illness (he is a little better today).

138

When news of my arrival at Glastonbury goes the rounds I am beset night and day to an extent that becomes unbearable. To carry on what I have to do, my etheric organism must be kept delicately adjusted: six months stay at Glaston and I should be a goner. How one shrinks from being made the object of a personality cult, and, speaking objectively, if WTP were to set up at Glastonbury people would elevate him to a state of indispensability and infallibility, followed inevitably when he went hence by a needless and harmful void.

This verbiage does not import that I long for reclusion or seclusion. But external human contacts need to be rationed, if it is wished that I should continue here for a while longer.

Grateful thanks for backing Clarice Toyne and Chris. Langlands in their valiant effort to prevent our C.W. property as an entity from being cut in two (perhaps forever) by a sale of the school buildings to Millfield. The present situation is one of touch and go.

My water thesis for Chalice Well has met with violent opposition in a certain quarter. A hand grenade beneath a certain chair may be the solution. In India and Persia, important springs are first lifted to form a fountain; the water then flows into a shallow marble-lined circular pool, on down terraces by an open conduit, and on into another shallow pool. And so on, seven times. The seventh pool is larger and deeper and usually surrounded by sacred trees and flowering shrubs. And it is only *there*, and nowhere else, that bathing and drinking and religious ritual are allowed. *Why?* So back me up!

I suppose I shall have to find up to £1000 for the new project, but am already expected to give £500 toward the £1500 for Chalice Well Trust to buy the school orchard and the two cottages. How far should one voluntarily go towards bare subsistence level?

Am amused by what you say as to my flirtations. Actually my trouble with the ladies is that the more I stand off, the stranger become their antics.

Glory be that your book proceeds. Look after yourself.

25.11.65

Paul Beard's review of *A.M.S.A.* in *Light* will please you I think. It is very perceptive. Leaving aside the ultra-orthodox respectables, I am sure your reputation has suffered no damage from your collaboration with WTP; in fact, admiration of R.L. has been much enhanced. I speak quite seriously and am thankful not to have let you down with a bump. I believe that the influence of the book will grow with time, and outlast the majority of current books on the Christian outlook.

Talking of personal losses: loss of my collections was nothing in comparison with the burning by bombs of all my diary records in 1944 at my Duke Street offices. As a result *The Silent Road* contains only the dregs of my life's experiences. To say nothing of historical letters from famous and infamous people. Curious that every attempt to destroy me during the war failed. Although on one occasion my clothes were stripped from me by blast. The *job* was what mattered, not me, and so the miracle happened.

How I agree with you! Modest daily service, no pretensions to spiritual stature, simple friendly humour and courage. These are to be striven for ahead of all else.

28.11.65

My very dear must be totally daft to find anything worth while in my scribbling. For me it is largely a letting-off of steam and therefore a very selfish indulgence.

140

My own beloved lady is both interested and pleased to watch the way R.L. and WTP have come together once more: to do a job of work and – by no means secondary – to enjoy each other's thoughts and feelings and the sparking of reactions. She reminded me that you are now fulfilling in many ways the role played earlier in my life by W. Lady Paget. The latter, however, with all her aristocratic charm, was an inveterate puller of strings, involving me on occasion in high politics, Court currents and international complexities. I suppose it was all necessary at the time, with personal access to the F.O. and the War House. Bless her heart even if now and then she still tries to pull a string whilst she should be letting go. The way this sad planet of ours carries on is no longer any business of hers.

30.11.65

Chalice Well must become international, and must also attract the younger generation. I have had to side-track too much stress on 'a spiritual healing centre', which would attract cranks mainly and create hostile attitudes locally.

4.12.65

Mark Twain was my friend and I helped him through the agony of losing his favourite daughter (drowned in her bath). Were he in incarnation now, I am sure he would contact me.

At the moment I feel that the C.W. group lacks a strong and balanced leader, prepared to *lead* and not expecting God to become their Chief Executive. The Divine Impulse must be made to work from *within* us; most people simply won't make their own decisions. D.R. would find all the money needed, were I in charge

141

of this undertaking. He has told me so. But, beyond sitting on any advisory panel formed, I cannot involve myself in running the show, at the sacrifice of what little peace and freedom now remains to me.

22.12.65

My very dear One, your visit cheered me up. Not that, fundamentally, I was seriously depressed (if very tired) but the vicious and uncalled-for attacks slanted at me recently have made me sad. All this will pass, and I look forward confidently to the coming of the primroses.

I hope you can get some rest and quiet times for the good progress of the book. Many people, often strangers, have 'phoned or written to thank you and me *very* enthusiastically and with deep emotion for our having conceived and produced *A.M.S.A.*

I understand how much you would like to recollect your past; both the favourable and the harrowing experiences. Often I wish I were unaware of all such matters, personal or otherwise. Knowledge of this kind *can* prove helpful, and also disconcerting. Silence is preferable, until one's lips are unsealed for a specific reason. All right! So tell me I am being evasive! As a matter of fact you yourself know far more about your own past than you think. And are influenced thereby to a considerable extent. Doors will open for you, and by and by WTP may help to set one or two of these wider.

Walburga turned up unexpectedly. And you are *right*: my Sanctuary visitor *is* whom you felt it was, and she is being helped by these visitations.

27.12.65

What a lovely piece of moss agate your very dear and generous self has sent me! You know my love of stones and crystals and semi-precious translucent metals. Contemplation of such lovely objects is a useful reminder of the many millions of years during which this planet was being prepared for the recent period in which sentient life has been able to inhabit it. Think of the ages through which fire, water, pressure, gases, earthquakes, intricate chemical processes and countless other tribulations combined to create such a wonder as this piece of moss agate! Such reflections keep one humble, and perhaps explain in their own way why man himself must undergo such a destiny of tribulation and sorrow in the course of his long evolution across eternity.

I hope your Christmastide went well and brought you rest as well as the enjoyment of watching the delight of your grandchildren. The Upper Room here was thronged by friends and visitors from far and wide in unseen realms. Also quite an important conference was in session there right through the night of Christmas Eve.

8.1.66

Jesus' attempt to form a small inner group of students failed. Once with five, later with only three, he formed a secret group with the help of an Essene expert; but the times were inopportune, the individuals unsuitable, the Forces of the Left immensely strong. Failure to create a united and harmonious whole, even from such a small group of people, led to disastrous events long before the Passover.

Down the ages, here and there, secret societies have played an important part in conserving truths that the multitude would only have destroyed. It may well be that this continues to be the case. But it seems to me that Westerners are not suited to secret societies. The floodgates of Truth have been opened as we enter a New Age: each dedicated seeker can now become aware of, and use, those segments of truth which can help him best to help others. In a sense therefore, in my view, secret societies are things of the past. Each one of us can and should become a secret society in himself. Too dogmatic? Well, I am open to correction.

143

When faced by the seeming inexplicable, do you go into your silence and let your inner mind release to your conscious self what it has to say? If so then what follows is already known to you: you had made preparations in thought for the way in which you intended to enlighten your friend on many of the facts of survival; hours before she slipped away your thoughts (and your love) had reached her telepathically and had been registered in a way which always functions when the end is near. This can be far more effective than the spoken word, and you have nothing to regret. Turn *inward* for confirmation of what I say.

I am at work in helping Solomon, a six-hundred-year-old oak tree near Lewes to renew its youth. In many ways a relief when compared with efforts to alleviate human ills, because Nature in itself and when friendly is far more forthcoming and grateful than humanity usually is. I hope this is not a catty remark.

My little genie tells me that by far the most important Dead Sea find is not yet found. And offered to show me where it is. But my questing days on these lines are over, and failure, though it has marked me, is a discipline no longer impossible to bear.

I daresay rumours are going the rounds about Avalon affairs. Certainly the most extraordinary things are being said about WTP in this connexion, in the west country. I can think of more suitable targets for these calumnies: fortunately I long ago gave up all concern for my reputation or the exposure of my alleged misdemeanours.

Public libraries, many of them, have waiting lists for *A Man Seen Afar*. The leaven is already more widely distributed than a sale to date of about 2,000 copies would suggest. On the whole I don't think we need regret our joint enterprise.

Every conceivable obstacle is being raised against me but I see no reason why the agreed plan for Chalice Well Trust and the School etc., should not go forward to fruition.

17.2.66

I am somewhat displeased with my little genie. For a purely personal end I desired a strong but slender and rather lengthy silver chain. 'Oh I can do better than that' interjected (into my thoughts) my L.G. Since it was a luxury I coveted, I told him to *hold off*. Three days later arrived by post (post mark obscured) a long very beautiful slender *gold* chain, one of considerable intrinsic value; the kind no doubt in use by ladies who wish to hang around their necks the likeness in miniature of the gentleman they adore. Naturally *no one* had any external access to what I had been thinking or wishing. This sort of thing must *stop*.

Yes M. is turning up trumps. Some are so anxious to help, and so remarkably capable only of hindering. Everyone (save you) thinks WTP can be pulled in every direction, being made, I suppose, of elastic. *Quite time* I went hence.

19.2.66

At last I am able to return copies of those Canadian sightings. P.L. has evaded the issue and imparted no fresh information to us. This is the attitude dictated by the Air Ministry, and one wonders what it is they fear? Why should serving airmen be muzzled?

Undoubtedly there are Intelligences within our planetary system who strongly object to our explosive interest in interplanetary space and in our raids upon the moon. Many supposed UFOs are no more than optical illusions, but others in fact are connected with a serious effort to discover what man is up to and what his spatial plans may be. A very few of these sightings are due to emissaries of the Solar Hierarchy who are carrying out important atmospheric activities with the object of trying to save life on our planet from colossal man-made disasters. How much of all this is known to American, French and British Air Ministries, whose files bulge with photographic and radiographic records of such visitations?

The warning given quite clearly in *A Message for the Coming Time* (though brought to the notice of certain high-ups) might as well have been uttered in the wilderness. What is the use of knowledge and experience gained over so many ages, if they cannot be shared? Yes, ignorance can be bliss and I wish I enjoyed the latter.

28.2.66

My very Dear, how *nice* for me but what a bore for you to come down all that way from town on Sunday, just for an indifferent cup of tea and a scone. The airing of my own problems took up far too much time. Whilst Sally's book is on the stocks would it not be arduous to undertake the scaffolding for another book on *A.M.S.A.* lines? Hugh Schonfield's account of the trial and crucifixion is banal and full of his own preconceived notions – e.g. his supposition concerning your Young Man could not be wider of the truth. Surely it is hardly worth commenting upon? Apart from any further specific questions and answers from you, your files (alas!) contain masses of data from which to quarry, when the project of a second book arises.

Enclosed notes are very scrappy and perhaps incoherent. I am trying to say that my main concern is with the influences which embrace the whole sweep of life-processes on and around this planet; not from the standpoint of centuries but of millennia.

Notes. Arising from our chat on Sunday, perhaps WTP's attitude towards human history should be summarized.

Speaking personally, then, I am far more of a Universalist than a Christian as generally understood. This is to say that I look out on life as a citizen of the spheres, very conscious of the cosmic background from which I derive; also, as an active entity within the Kingdoms of Nature, and not simply a being confined to human conditions. The whole eternal sweep of manifested Life, visible and invisible, is my concern and is as much me as I am it.

Does this statement suggest egotism? In fact the very opposite would be nearer the truth. The glimpses in *A Man Seen Afar* in the main reflect the objective but sympathetic attitude of a Universalist towards the birth throes of a new and very special chapter in human history, and in Him who wrote and inspired this first chapter. My role, as so often before and since, was less that of a participant than an onlooker.

It has been suggested that an effort should be made to recover further glimpses from the same point in human history and from the same geographical location. This may be possible, and might be valuable, but as a Universalist it does not concern me very deeply either way. It is the cosmic background, and the emergence of the eternal verities from that background, which do.

In this context the Christian story, not yet two thousand years old, is an incident of note but a very minute fragment of a 'film' that has been unrolling for many millions of years past. What I am trying to say is this: whilst willing to add to the glimpses of Jesus' life on earth should this be necessary and prove possible, I am far more at home in writing about verities of universal application, ageless in character, the re-statement of which could have a special value for our day. For instance, on the theme 'God is Love'; or on the Archangels; these are as applicable to followers of other faiths (or of none) as they are to Christians. Our need is to widen vision, to realize more clearly the universality of all life processes over the aeons and not only as manifested on this speck of dust we call Earth.

We need to become *aware* of our part in the great panorama. This is what I mean by the word 'universality', recognition of the oneness of all creation with its Creator: an idea hardly to be expressed in words, and those words incomprehensible save to the very few. Nevertheless it is questions of this depth that can bring into being answers which could well form the foundations upon which the next chapter in our history will be based. If further glimpses into the life and teaching of the Christ through Jesus could help to strike the note of universality about which I am writing, then an effort should be made to recapture such glimpses. If not, such glimpses though interesting could have little relevance to what is of fundamental importance in the present context.

1.3.66

I have checked up on my own movements around the time of the Crucifixion. Surely I have recorded these? Otherwise, the absence of first-hand glimpses of that momentous time, in *A.M.S.A.*, must seem strange. When I got home from my visit to the house of the Upper Room late at night, I found a message awaiting me from the overseer of our property in Syria. (Above Baalbek in the hills.) My presence was requested because a strange blight had descended on our groves of olives. Next day I set off there, and was gravely concerned with the languishing condition of the trees and the soil beneath them. I tried to banish the thought that here was some sinister omen: I mean a sort of fellow-feeling with their kind on the Mount of Olives. Anyway I was up there for two weeks working out remedies, then left for Alexandria on business, by sea from Aleppo.

Some time later and when I was back at home in Jerusalem, the tragedy and its aftermath had begun to slide into history; the stories were contradictory, charged with emotion and surmise, hence I have not even reliable hearsay to go on. What I do relate in *A.M.S.A.* about this period is based mainly on a clairvoyant interpretation of auric and hearsay impressions (a reconstruction). As you know, the glimpses into Kopul's and your Young Man's mind, and the Garden incidents, were not first-hand *seeing* on my part.

A.M.S.A. It takes an expert reader to distinguish glimpses which are the seer's memories of direct participation from those of clairvoyance, or inward seeing from a distance. In the Garden scene, for instance, the clairvoyant beholder is reading the Akashic Record almost as soon as human events are inscribed upon it. Instances of his (my) physical presence include the walk with Jesus in the Judean hills and the rescue by the Jordan of the wounded hare. There is a third and intermediate category in what I term the 'riding of the mind' of various individuals, such as Kopul, and occasionally Mary of Magdala; in which cases the inward eye is actually accompanying the physical persons concerned.

If I am asked to delve into the actual events of Calvary and the Tomb a very arduous study and translation of the Akashic Records is required, and here arises a problem: great happenings infused with deep cosmic significance are recorded in the 'Golden Book', a kind of spiritual counterpart of the Akashic, by no means easy of access, and records moreover so profoundly symbolic as to be almost beyond interpretation by the human mind. The prescience and the direct influence of the Christos, going back before the dawn of time, permeates and protects this volume. A comparatively minute section of its contents deals with the Christos' overshadowing on earth of the Master Jesus. The external aspect of that story is easily available in the Akashic Record, but to secure a really valid interpretation, including the cosmic realities behind human events associated with supreme Masters and Saviours of the Race, it is essential to study the Golden Book *with* the general Record, and to do this with the perception of the Initiate. Is such a task worth attempting? Silence, serenity, time are needed. Perhaps I can judge how much is involved if you will send me a list of your queries.

Looking back, I think it was natural that having returned from the house of the Upper Room 'filled with forebodings' I should seek with my mind's eye to follow when Jesus and those around him left the house and went on into the garden. However I was not sufficiently involved to postpone my departure for Syria. Useless now to speculate as to why I did not remain in Jerusalem at all costs.

A.M.S.A. The rhythm in those days was powerful but its vibration was slower than is the case today. To move out of one rhythm into another takes some doing, and sometimes leads to the jangle of falling between two stools. Thank your lucky stars that you are not called to move about in 'time', and so can concentrate on the needs of 'today'. To catch flashes of experience belonging to past incarnations does not call for a change of rhythm unless one wants to re-live the events. Better, for most, to leave well alone until qualified to operate safely in these ways.

Tibet is no place for you now, a tragic distracted sorrowful country where true spiritual inspiration has been stamped into the ground. A very high ranking Ringode who secreted invaluable parchments in which I am interested was killed escaping into Kashmir, and the secret of their hiding place has gone with him. Another Abbot who left his monastery and two thousand students, now in England with some dozen close followers, actually sought asylum with us at Chalice Well. I think however we can house them permanently on an estate in Banffshire. Strong nerves are needed in Tibet now, even by visitors out of the body.

A good deal of what I tell you is a kind of metaphysical chit chat, transitory in value. Comments on the current psychic scene will soon be outdated in any case. The trouble is that most people are fascinated by the phenomenal and have no desire to look deeper.

Passion Week as usual brings incessant emphasis by our mentors on the wickedness of our sins; cries for mercy, forced contrition, sermons on blood sacrifice and its efficacy on our behalf. When are we going to stand up like men? Enough of all this wormlike supplication. I accept responsibility for what I am and what I do, and I'm fully prepared to take the consequences.

5.4.66

Sitting on the rim of this sad world with my feet dangling over the edge, ready to spring when the summons comes, I find the vision of human suffering almost overwhelming. Our dark nights of the soul, insignificant by comparison with that through which passed Jesus the great Initiate, may seem to us undeserved and futile too; but this is not so. As we look up, refusing to be dismayed, and going our way with courage, we are helping more than we know to reduce the great woe of the world and to enlighten the general darkness.

What follows may seem recondite: man on this planet stands at the point where effects manifest. Causes are not generated here. We combine various effects and think as a result that we are causative creatures, but that is not our function in this our primary school state. All effects pass away as the shadows of night, and this includes all our personal sorrows and misbehaviour. Causation is in higher hands and the Creative Will is carrying out its supreme purposes all the time. If we do the best we know, there is nothing to fear, and Light will shine on the path and bring us peace and understanding.

7.4.66

It would be disturbing if our Avalon venture were not beset by trials and tribulations. Such a power house is free to all, and it is natural that our friends of the Left should avail themselves of it in the effort to stem progress. In due course and when 'defeated' their energies will join ours. We are too prone to wear dark glasses.

By the way, my remark about the summons does not portend its imminence. I am taking off and on regularly. Part of my job is to report in high places (causative regions) on effects at the human level. And at times to bring about changes of rhythm for the alleviation of material conditions. It is the habit of a lifetime, but tell it not in Athens (or should it be Thebes?).

May your Avalon/St. Davids pilgrimage bring pleasure and inspiration!

24.4.66

People of mediumistic tendency have auras which attract intelligences good, bad and indifferent, and these may enter into human conditions even to the point of physical manifestation by means of the scent such an aura emits. Had you been travelling alone the other day you might well have felt no more than a sense of depression or unease, but a medium's presence in the car enabled the semi-materialization of an influence that was frightening.* It was unfortunate the energy behind the incident was not benign, as it might equally have happened to be. As I wrote to Barry, we need to learn how to become lightning conductors. Mediumship has always played a part in human affairs and it may be that on balance the good effects outweigh the dangers, illusions and emotional disturbances it can bring: I point no moral, even if as you know my bias is in favour of communion rather than communication. I hope my comments may not be taken to imply anything derogatory to B. or any other seeker on the path who may have been born with a particular astral constitution.

* The 'influence' or 'incident' here referred to was terrifying – best not described in detail – and happened on our return journey from our St. David's pilgrimage. Whether or not 'it' was attracted by B's aura, she dealt with it with a courage and spiritual resourcefulness I shall never forget.

The rush to get away! What a boring business it always is! May all blessings and good fortune attend you! I will keep in touch so far as my own hectic life here and elsewhere will allow.

The Sharmas never told me that their soirée was to be an occasion and I arrived all unprepared for the ten ill-assorted individuals invited to meet me. There was no chance to discuss the Etna solution research project. I wish I had stayed at home.

Glastonbury. The much-lauded new housekeeper turns out to be another medium, open to every current from the astral and emotionally highly unstable. Someone having told her in advance that Glastonbury was full of 'evil' she has been duly complaining of nightmares and astral 'attacks'. These I investigated and found that her bedroom contained a good deal of karmic debris, as do most old houses, but that her reaction was excessive in the circumstances; and now of course rumours have spread alleging 'black magic' and the rest. No peace on earth for this wicked one.

Pay my respects to the Statue of Liberty* and assure her of my prayers. Long-suffering ladies are ever my concern. So, if you come into this category (and in any case) *take advantage.*

25.6.66

My very dear, Yes, I know it's been a long gap, but you have never left my thoughts and my love. For fourteen days I allowed personal letters to go unanswered: legal problems connected with the Tor School takeover, arranging to house sixty Canadian youths and others early in August; and the same for thirty diggers later in the month; unearthing a trained secretary to come in every other day – and much else. However all is now running more smoothly down there and visitors flock in and in.

* I went as President of the English Centre to the International PEN Congress in New York, in May, 1966.

I have been obliged to spend far more time and energy than usual in Borderland, hedging and ditching the dark jungles that result largely from man's misuse of his mental and emotional powers down here: trying to let some light in, with a devoted band of helpers. We have been enlarging our own Rescue Station and building a much needed new one as well. Watching arrivals from earth brings home forcibly the fact that most dwellers there are little more than children, morally and spiritually speaking; the leaven of reasonably evolved souls now in incarnation is dangerously low. I have told what Powers I can reach that unless a considerable number of really evolved beings can be persuaded to reincarnate here well before the end of the century, life on this planet can't be salvaged. It is in the lap of the Gods. After all it is their concern before it is mine, who am in fact no more than a visitor here.

29.6.66

Lucifer. At intervals the Ego, the essential spirit of this great Being, returns for rest and refreshment to his own high place in the Heavens. He did so after our two recent great wars. His mission never ceases, even during such withdrawals; and of course he commands a great company in his service at all times. His Testing Mission is by no means over, nor would he seek release before completing the great task. Cosmic processes of this order occupy aeons of human time and we cannot compute when the end will be. The present turning-point in our planet's history should bring a lightening of his labours well within the next two thousand years.

Get into the mood to understand and sympathize with Lucifer and his fiery hosts. Part of their mission in fact is to cleanse by fire. See Lucifer as a colleague, send him your love, offer up a prayer – not to him, but with him – for the success of his mission among men; and for his triumphant return whence he came. He was *not* 'cast out of Heaven', but descended into our midst of his free will and to his own sacrifice. He can only rise out of our darkness when *we* are ready and able to rise with him.

Cheer up! Nothing unpleasant lasts beyond its essential usefulness. Whereas love and harmony, joy and strength are our birthright and eternal.

7.7.66

As to your queries about WTP, what can I say that will be of value or of any interest, to you or to anyone? I don't think much is likely to be revealed of his identity whilst he is still here. Later on, going through his papers you may catch glimpses. WTP is *on loan* to this planet, as he has been on a number of past occasions. He will be in no hurry to return, having immense tasks awaiting him elsewhere, but by 'immense' I do not mean to imply any particular degree of evolutionary eminence.

In any case attention should be given, if given at all, to the grains of wheat that may be found here and there among the chaff of his writings.

16.7.66

Very dear one, I have been obliged to cut down my writing for the time being to below twenty letters a day, most of which are business, or replies to urgent calls. It has been necessary too to withdraw somewhat in order to remain perceptive to calls from outside this planet. I have only been in London once all the week but am due up on Monday next, when the last meeting of the Tor School Board is being held.

It would be really nice were you able to be present on 20th July, but I don't think you care for crowds, and anyway I shall be torn in two. My talk to the Companions will be more important than usual, but I may be able to make a transcript. Subsequently I may have to become incommunicado for a week or two, may even go abroad.

155

I do trust you are feeling more yourself? Your letters recently have recounted many woes and worries without revealing that you are making use of the magic remedy, always in your hands, so simple and so easily overlooked: count your blessings and discount your woes. Make a list of the many reasons you have to give thanks; your good home, loyal friends, freedom from poverty, opportunities to help others, growing spiritual perception and much else. *Never* cease to give thanks, even when clouds look dark. Persist night and day and close all other doors. Then the magic will begin to work.

26.8.66

Two other cars were stolen from the Sloane Square area on the evening when you lost yours. It was not easy to disentangle the wires therefore. However, yours was taken by a youngster, not a professional car thief. He was not difficult to panic but he could not find the place from which he had pinched it and so left it as near as he could remember. Apart from any damage caused by amateur driving the car should be in good condition. I think this lad has now learned his lesson and was given a good fright.

The Tor dig has been rewarding but it would take too long now to give details. The press has shown keen interest. On the whole all went well and a new and better chapter is opening for our Chalice Well adventure. I cannot speak now or yet on the mission I was asked to fulfil esoterically. But I don't think the dangers entailed will cling to me for long. Rather sad that during it my Greek intaglio ring disappeared as if into thin air, on my finger one moment and then . . . gone. So far I have made no effort to recover it because I don't know the reason for its being taken.

It was a lovely day and the gardens were perfect. About eighty Companions came, of whom perhaps six or seven took my meaning. I told them a little about the way in which certain Essene seers were able to perceive Jesus' entry into the realm of human consciousness, some seventy years before he incarnated. And also to pick up the gist of the teaching he was preparing to give. And to inscribe some of it on their Community's scrolls, well before A.D. And how the Coming One has now entered within our atmosphere, so that it is possible to predict the lines on which his teaching is likely to run, should he take bodily form. I think little of this registered, to judge from lack of comment. However the demand subsequently for the less complete text has tended to exceed the supply.

27.8.66

It turns out that the ring I 'lost' was used as a kind of lightning conductor to preserve my bodily life. A noble effort no doubt, using a technique unfamiliar to me, to divert an immense complex of uncontrolled energy. I hardly think this successful intervention was worth while: I am expendable.

The object of the recent exercise on my part was the establishment of a clear channel through which instruction and illumination could be *safely* conveyed to human consciousness. A titanic task and not yet completed, one moreover that has had a shattering bodily effect on me. One consolation is that, when bodily staggered to this extent, in some strange way my faculty of vision is enhanced. But I ought not to dwell on the personal aspect, of no moment whatsoever.

Stimulation of conscience, with an ingredient of panic, was all that was necessary to restore your car to you. I am not surprised to hear of mystification on the part of the police.

8.9.66

When lying in the snow below Etna's crater I was told to go forward with my quest for a cancer cure, but that only seeds could be sown and that fruit from such seeds could not be expected during my present sojourn on earth.

Which reminded me of that other Quest, still to be fulfilled by others. In both, personal motives were wholly absent, and gain not looked for. Why failure? Yet this I have had to accept.

Peter* needs someone congenial and clear-sighted to share his thoughts and feelings. We must try to lift him out of this concentration upon his immediate circumstances, help him to seek and find wider vision. We are seeing a cleaning of the karmic slate. Peter's brother, by consent and not necessity, skipped an earthly incarnation in order to give Peter the chance to 'catch up', so that they could then go forward together on equal terms. Can love and comradeship go further than this? Meanwhile he is helping Peter through his valley of the shadow, to be followed by a very joyful reunion and the start of a new and inspiring chapter together.

Yes, of course these twins have crossed your path many times here and elsewhere, and will do so again, in circumstances of splendid augury and mutual service. Peter and you are linked from the past in ways that never excluded his brother, and you were within their life-orbit during the Louis XIV period. But you know all this so why do I carry coals to Newcastle?

15.9.66

If the urge persists then Peter M. should come over here, for the solace of your love and presence. Certainly his brother sees no objection and will be available here as there.

Twins are of two kinds, ordinarily linked in this way more or less casually for a single life on earth but, far more rarely, and as with P.M., the link goes back for many lives here and elsewhere, and is destined to hold indefinitely. In fact a time might come (but this is not for his ears) when by mutual consent the two could become one for the purpose of carrying out a very special task.

* Peter Morris, a dear friend, at whose death, after many months of suffering, I was present. For years he had made his home in Mexico, but came to England for treatment for cancer, – useless, alas. But he did make a very important link with WTP before his death.

It is for WTP to direct you to the Source of all solutions, the Christos within. As you know, I have work to do not easily carried out by others. Regard me more as a specialist to be consulted when real urgency arises, rather than a G.P. always on tap. Otherwise where will you be when the person disappears? You wrote recently that I am constantly in your thoughts; whereas what I try to convey should be in the forefront. You know that my deep love is yours now and at all times and that my comradeship is sure, you have my help and my guidance, but remember the One who calls for awakenment within.

On the proposed new translation of the Bible by *Time and Life* experts, I doubt they are capable of the translucent interpretation of the New Testament that is needed. Theologians forget that Jesus intended his church to be founded on the simplicity of Peter's character, whereas the task fell to Paul, forerunner of all the political ecclesiastics. May the Revealer of the Word for our time, and those who prepare his way, restore true spiritual simplicity in their expression of eternal Truth.

Bless you!

20.9.66

You ask what sparked off my comment about reliance. Probably it was that urgent postscript of yours, asking protection for the Devenish adventure (and sounding rather troubled). Were you not aware that full protection was available to you, from the Christos within, absolutely equal to this and all occasions? Oh dear! I grow sanctimonious. . . . To link Light centres through pilgrimage and prayer is to give great help to the Guardians of such centres. The requisites are simplicity, faith and purity of purpose. When other factors intervene, such as the notion that one is Michael's specially chosen mouthpiece etc., then dangers arise. If you are not fully satisfied that all forms of astralitis are absent from such ventures, then you should not participate.

159

The re-kindling of Michael centres at home and overseas, by pilgrimage, prayer and silence, is fully in accord with the wishes of the Revealer of the Word. In fact one of the purposes of my life since 1910 has been just this.

In 1904 Glastonbury was dead, or anyway in coma, spiritually speaking. In 1905 I found Iona in similar condition, benumbed. In 1906 Devenish was riddled with unattractive elementals. The first two have now been brought back to life, beacons re-kindled. Not so Devenish, in fact when I went there first (1905) it was made clear to me that the cleansing process would be long and dangerous and would call for very expert handling. I have some experience in this field, having taken part in re-kindling some twenty-five centres, in our own Islands and right across Europe, the Middle East and Africa. The technique calls for knowledge and selfless dedication, with complete immunity from attendant astral influences.

Let us try to get this Devenish business into perspective. Early in the century I found this centre overrun by hostile elementals, and it was evident that unlike Avalon and Iona, Devenish was not ripe for re-illuming. All that could be done *then* was to restrain the adverse forces until the time should come to release and transmute them in an evolutionary direction. When I was last there, it was clear that the recent visit of well-meaning exorcists had resulted in the premature release of these energies; so it was necessary to re-confine them, an arduous and dangerous job. Then recently and almost by a side wind I was told that B. had received instructions from high Michael sources to visit Devenish on a mission of her own. I was not consulted, nor was I impressed to intervene, but to leave B's freewill to demonstrate the value of her guidance. And so these semi-malignant and partially intelligent forces are once more at large, and once more must be confined.

Some chink in M's armour resulted in his becoming a casualty. (Just as you nearly became one at the end of a previous pilgrimage to the west country and Wales.)

Thank you for a delightful lunch and your welcome company to Hampstead. An interesting vignette which took me back to pre-1914 Turkey, Southern Russia and the Balkans. The Gagarins were feudal chieftains centuries before the upstart Romanovs appeared on the scene; hence our hostess's comparative indifference to the tragic end of Tsarist Russia. There is a vast nature power house on the N.E. slopes of the Elburz mountains, not far from Amula, deep in the immense forests that slope down to the Caspian. Its function is the generation of energy by which the planet remains on course, to avoid toppling, one of seven similar centres situated at strategic points around the globe. The Gagarin property in Turkestan is nowhere near this centre, but has a subtle link with it and so arouses my interest. The conversion of the Elburz (Amula) power house into a Light Centre has been one of my lifelong preoccupations, and is of vast importance to the welfare of all life on this planet.

Peter M. You are doing all you can, and we will hope that his brother can get through to him sufficiently to give the needed impetus in these last stages of his present life.

Glad Peter M. is more comfortable. Your love and presence are proving of incalculable service to him.

Francis H. has just departed after years of invalidism. He has left me (for the Chalice Well Trust) his diamond-studded pectoral cross, his Abbot's diamond-studded ring, a silver monstrance, his unique green scarab ring and a necklace. What *can* the C.W.T. do with such things – which would of course be highly valued elsewhere, say by the Benedictine Abbey of Downside? There is no proviso in his Will to prevent their sale, but I suppose he hoped they could be preserved at C.W.? But *à quoi bon*? The scarab ring I covet, as it was in my possession once long ago, before it came into its present setting.

When I was twelve I developed a craving for Scotch shortbread (a taste I still retain). At fourteen, my parents told me that when I was eleven Robert McVitie had offered to adopt me, educate me in Edinburgh and make me his heir. I knew nothing of this at the time, or I would have cleared off to Edinburgh on my own. A millionaire foster-father should not have been discounted, especially one who was lonely, attractive, a fine character who evidently felt a close tie with the strange youngster I then was. My mind had matured well beyond my years at eleven and I was already engaged on other-worldly missions and pursuits. My affinity with Robert McV. was strong and my attachment to my father very frail. My parents' refusal, without consulting me, seemed unforgivable.

15.11.66

'Unforgivable' because at eleven I was more or less grown up and an independent entity. 'I am not a chattel', was the feeling uppermost in my mind just then. My father was of the Norman type with some Anglo-Saxon blood. The de la Poles had been to the Crusades and my father himself was a crusader for unpopular causes. My mother came from Owen Tudor stock, later mixed with the Evans/Wansbrough strain, and marriage with my father was a test for two opposing temperaments.

Glad to hear of P.M's progress and freedom from pain and of all you have been able to do for him. Do you ever reminisce together about the fifteenth to seventeenth centuries in France and Italy?

162

The Vatican has secured a very important Dead Sea scroll but refuses to allow it to be examined by outsiders. Its contents are causing bewilderment to its Jesuit translators.

17.11.66

You may remember that my wallet was lost or stolen on the London Underground, a month ago? The use of my customary technique for recovery has had surprising results. Two days ago, the treasury notes that were in it arrived by post on their own and anonymously. A later post brought the rest of the contents, also anonymously. Finally the empty wallet materialized. Yet when I tried the same technique in connexion with my intaglio ring lost at Glastonbury, I was suddenly called off using it.

I am alarmed by the number of people who go berserk if they don't get a weekly personal letter from me. Something must be done to loosen these dependencies before nature abruptly stops such material forms of contact.

Links with the past (this in answer to your query). I should need first to get inside the aura of each of your grandchildren. Then to find out whether such a search was permitted. Then, if permitted, to spend hours – perhaps days – isolated more or less whilst picking up the threads and following them both back and forth. I cannot operate by hey presto methods. But you are in touch with mediums you trust and surely they can provide the indications you seek? If great need arose, no doubt I could act, but *does* urgent need exist?

The regalia I told you of has now reached me. Thirteen of the diamonds in his cross and two of his rings are perfect and must be very valuable. A large pearl set in the middle of the cross (*what* a mistake!) has lost its lustre. From his two other rings, both Ancient Egyptian, I discover that he had been dabbling for years in a form of magic beyond his capacity to control. Hence, no doubt, his years of crippledom. The larger of the rings, an inscribed cornelian, still possesses almost unbelievable sexual potency. The other, an Osiric scarab, still has attached to it a semi-tame elemental, not a high intelligence, but begs me not to detach him from his home in the ring. 'I have lost touch with my group and if you send me away I shall soon lose the identity which contact with the ring has given me', etc., etc. My own genie is of course more advanced and hoping soon to be promoted from vegetable status to the Kingdom of the Air; whereas this poor solitary mite* is linked with the mineral world and has no wish for promotion or change.

Well I won't jabber on any longer, so boring for you.

7.12.66

Psychic fact and fiction are inextricably mingled in both the Cup and the Quest stories. How to re-establish the central thread of truth?

The Quest must be carried on by someone of the correct calibre on *this* side as is the case in parallel on the other side. From about 1922 to 1940 the Q. group of five were constantly told that a sixth and vital member was missing, and unless found *in time* Q. fulfilment was endangered in this generation. He was referred to as X. and sometimes as M., taken to mean 'missing'. He was said to be English upper class, well off, something of a playboy, keen on travel, unmarried; emotionally unsatisfied, and unless con-tacted destined to miss the major part of his vocation. On these slender clues we searched high and low – London, Paris, Italy and the Near East; and were advised of his past links with Byzantium and its rulers. For which reason I think he would recognize Helias' description of the House of Justinian. But he has not been found, and now all Q. members save WTP have departed to other spheres.

* The fate of this 'poor solitary mite' continues to haunt me!

164

The Quest. The latest intimation is that P.M. should be offered a sight and study of Q. Records and photos, but that no transfer of threads should be placed before him at this juncture. No commitments on either side. Agreed?

A question constantly posed to me is this: 'Apart from the Joseph of Arimathea story, why do you feel that Chalice Well will be used as a platform for a renewal of the Christ message?' My reply: 'It is not a question of will be or otherwise; Chalice Well *is already* being used in this way, and will continue so to be used.' Naturally, few at present will feel able to accept that statement.

Quest. I will fit my dates to yours. Can P.M. manage stairs? I cannot remove the Cup just now from its place in the sanctum, the Energies around it are engaged on vital work.

I felt it wiser to allow events to unroll before alerting you to details of the sixth member of the Quest. If P.M. naturally responds, well and good. Otherwise let it go, and certainly no pressure must be used. The responsibility if incurred includes that of deciding to whom the thread should be passed on. Apart from this and perhaps a visit to the spot, if health permits, and a study of the plans and documents, it is unlikely that other activities will fall to his lot in the weaving of the Q. pattern on earth. Meanwhile he must be free to make up his own mind.

Very sorry to hear of the setback and I think a trip down here may prove too exhausting. I would make a special journey to London (with the Cup) to meet P.M. *chez vous* somewhere around the

New Year. I don't think you have scale drawings of the under-ground passages, their exits, extent and very many photographs and plans?

My brother Alex seems to think that P.M. is 'a Q.-associate' from the past, and should be re-linked 'before coming here'. Alex knew of P.M. and once nearly contacted him in Mexico City, where A. spent the last twenty years of his life. But they moved in different circles and A. himself became a recluse, deeply involved in theosophical occultism. He was not a Q. member, but under-stood the implications and is far more interested now than then.

Christmastide 1966

Your Christmas will be overshadowed with grief and the sense of impending separation. *But* it will also be relieved by the knowledge of a great and loving service you have been blessed to render to a great and faithful friend in the hour of his departure and his need. Also you have acted as the means by which a Quest link was forged, thus enabling P.M. to take his rightful part from now on in Quest affairs.

Reunion with his brother will bring them both joy, and they will now progress together to the fulfilment of their joint destiny, with a clean karmic slate and a splendid vista ahead.

Among much else this includes full participation in the Quest mission, which extends through several spheres and is by no means confined to the activities of Justinian times on earth. For over two hundred years now I have been working towards a special objective, patiently waiting for the right blend of conditions to mature. This concerns the creation of a Research University which I am now helping to build on a specially selected site, where (to use symbolic language) Light and Darkness coincide. The Staff drawn from many quarters will be supervised by a Master of the Seventh Degree. There are two ends in view: The first, to train preparers of the Way, for work both in incarnation and in the intermediary realms, with the ability to move to and fro. The second, research into better methods for thinning the veils between the third, fourth and fifth dimensions of being. Many pioneers in pscyhic communication, who have resided on our earth during the past 125 years or so, are joining the staff and nearly all are known to me personally. I hope to arrange later for P.M. and his brother to have the opportunity of graduating here. And to arrange for *you* to do likewise, in time to come when given your freedom to do so, should the urge arise.

I am not entrusting to the post a very modest gift which will I hope be ready to hand over to you in the New Year.

As ever your very loving comrade W.

6.1.67

My very dearest R., it always fills me with humble amazement when those who visit me report such effects as those which you describe. Certainly it is *not* WTP who is responsible, save as a very imperfect intermediary. However, my amazement is tinged with gratitude.

The Egyptian beads* date mainly from the 18th Dynasty, but a few belong to the 17th and 16th. Several of them are inbued with the aura of Akhenaton's lovely and devoted wife and comrade.† They have been back together at least twice, in comparatively humble but significant circumstances. He is now on a level with Zoroaster, both inhabitants of the solar planet: each planet possesses its double or interior reflection within which life in myriad forms evolves and progresses, and in many ways influences life outwardly throughout our system. Yes, my permanent home is within the solar planet, but I have several homes elsewhere. *Not* that this signifies exalted rank or any special degree of advancement.

* TP's Xmas present to me.
† Nefertiti.

Walburga's end in a 'pillar of fire' is told I think in *The Silent Road* but without revealing her identity. She came to say how do you do? to you, very affectionately, when you were here the other day. And *inter alia* backed up your idea about my next step in the Quest. How can I resist such authoritative instructions from the pair of you, who were once (and again will be) comrades and fellow workers? In any case you must concede that WTP exercises very careful discrimination in his choice of buddies? Both W. and G.T.C. were famous for their beauty; and their inborn charm was so authentic that it lasted all their lives. These splendid qualities are yours in the present tense, whereas your two predecessors only came into my life at a time when the sun was beginning to set on their earthly spans.

People write urging me to appoint a successor to take over the Chalice Well Trust (as leader), saying I should nominate my choice in my will. I don't believe in dead-hand tactics even if an obvious choice were available. Materially speaking, the C.W.T. is now on a sound footing. And the magazine has brought in many new Companions. If support for the Trust depends on WTP's presence then such interest can only be skin-deep. My problem is to find younger people to carry on the work.

Our next task is to create an exact replica of Our Lord's Room within the Upper Room at Little St. Michael's; simple, as authentic as possible, and no ecclesiastical trimmings. Some keynote has to be struck by the autumn – this, or a book.

Are you staying put at Little Eden for some time? If so I hope conditions will be good for serenity and the book.

P.M. has now been allowed to survey the whole of his recent incarnation, to begin to learn its lessons and to emerge gradually from the land of regrets. He has conveyed to you (telepathically?) his *deep* gratitude for all you did to help him across and for your lifelong friendship.

A good article on the R.C. turmoil in last Sunday's *Observer*. The paradox is that mature leaders are leaving the Church at the very time when many youngsters are joining it in search of security. Years ago when a determined effort was made to get WTP in, a young and persuasive priest told me, 'They (i.e. the Vatican) feel that you will be less dangerous inside than out.' What danger had they in view, I wonder? The Quest . . . ?

17.3.67

How exasperating can my little genie be? He knew of my quest of a table to resemble that of the Last Supper. As you know, the owner of that little house on the outskirts of Jerusalem was a master carpenter, an expert craftsman in wood carving. He had made the table himself for use sacramentally at the annual Passover ceremonies in his upper room. These were attended by about a dozen friends and relatives, including of course his wife and her unmarried sister, and in due course by his two children, a boy and a girl. He was instinctively a seer, and when making the table 'knew' it was destined to a use beyond his normal comprehension. The table top was of olive wood, two sections of lovely grain finely laminated, and the under carriage and simply carved but finely proportioned legs were made from yew, but lightish in colour: dimensions about seven feet by two and three-quarters. Well, my genie's instructions were: 'Not far from the hotel you frequent in London you can find what you want, as nearly as is possible today, in a cellar.' So on Thursday last I prowled around the side streets adjoining St. Ermins and finally espied a kind of furniture repository. In I went and made enquiries.

'What you seek is virtually impossible to provide anywhere

today, and especially if the table must not be made of oak.' However I was led down a long labyrinth into a series of cellars, and by and by espied in a dark recess the very table held for so long in view of my mind's eye. Dimensions almost exact, very simple in texture and design with an aura of dedication. Were my eyes deceiving me? Lights were put on and the table's beauty revealed. The top was made of a light coloured fruit wood, probably cherry, two long sections laminated together. The under-carriage and superbly but simply carved legs were made of *yew*. Early seventeenth century and perhaps made in our own west country.

Then of course came the shock: price £650, being unique or nearly so *vide* the seller. I sat down on a stool nearby (one very like those I seek) and wept, metaphorically speaking. Then in fury I turned on my genie, telling him he must have known my limit was £280. 'What has the price to do with me? Don't expect me to solve all your problems for you. I can but do my best,' and off he went.

If the cash were available we should not be justified in such an outlay.

28.3.67

Ena Twigg. Excellent, and I wish I had seen and heard her on T.V. She must be a remarkable woman, helped by the fact that one who overshadows her is very clairvoyant; which is not the case with the majority of Guides.

I have been asked to advise on the strange way in which compasses on ships and aircraft on occasion deviate without known cause. A number of air crashes have been due to this, and more will follow. The causes are complex, but they include the interference caused by all these magnetic man-made metallic objects now hurtling around our upper atmosphere. Nuclear power stations emanate radio-active substances which create magnetic disturbances through which compasses are affected. Easier to diagnose the cause than discover the remedy. Science without vision is the very devil, but *who* recognizes this? I have arranged for research on the problem, of a kind that will compel the attention of authority. Meantime disasters will continue.

10.4.67

Congratulations that *the* book is now complete: a weight off your time and mind.

It may sound a counsel of perfection but remember that the more one lives, in thought and in imagination, within the spirit of oneself, the less the outer fabric creaks and cracks. Now don't chaff the antique WTP. Do as I tell you.

As to what I wrote about Akhenaton, you are probably aware that the strange phenomenon of proxy incarnations is a fact; even if a very rare one? There are occasions when Initiates, still in the process of human evolution, find it inconvenient to return bodily to earth. Perhaps they are engaged on important tasks elsewhere, yet wish to 'see' into our world at times in connexion with these tasks. On such occasions someone is chosen who is being drawn back into incarnation in fulfilment of his own karma, and permission is sought and given for him to be directly over-shadowed by the Initiate in question (say Akhenaton) who thus relates what he is doing elsewhere with temporal experience here. (Badly expressed, because there is a mystery involved which is not to be quite encompassed by words.)

However the greater number of those who affirm that they themselves embody important historic or religious figures from the past (or even are overshadowed by such) are indulging in wishful thinking: because this direct overshadowing is rare, and only happens when the need is great, for high evolutionary purposes. This does not rule out the many cases where those incarnating are in fact living within the auric streams of radiation proceeding from this or that great Being who once lived amongst us; but the direct connexion which I call incarnation by proxy is rare and different. Akhenaton has used the method twice.

171

As to the difficulty of returning to earth experienced by those whose mummified previous bodies still exist, there may be exceptions: I know of two cases where the attempt was made, and in both the individuals arrived stillborn.

Of course, everyone is overshadowed by the Christos, even if most of us allow that Influence to remain asleep and unrecognized.

12.4.67

One more note about Akhenaton. The procedure described enables the overshadower to tune in whenever he so desires to the life and activities of the overshadowed. He can follow all that the latter feels and thinks and does, in a way that is almost first-hand. He can be aware of the contents of the newspapers read, of exchanges with other people, spectacles viewed in theatres, cinemas and the rest, and every detail which could have a bearing on his task elsewhere, no matter from which realm he is operating. A very fascinating phenomenon to watch.

27.4.67

Yours from London reached me on return from Glastonbury. There is a Presence already apparent in the Upper Room, now taking on its destined shape and atmosphere. As a gesture to mark its inauguration I intend finding funds to provide an Indian village with water; this also as an expression of thankfulness for our own ever-flowing supply from our pure spring. Would you like to be part of this?

Due to a needless leakage of the fact that St. George's Day is my birthday I was swamped with callers, letters and 'phone calls, which left me little time for all I had to do down there. The

172

gardens are looking breathlessly beautiful and good progress is being made in all directions. I return to be swamped anew, so this is only to send you a further supply of my love and devotion. Rest all you can!

7.5.67

Strange how many good people long for extinction at bodily death. They won't get it, but if they *will* strongly enough they will pass into a coma from which it will take them a long time to wake. Then good friends come along and gently rouse the sleeping ones, who soon are grateful to be alive again.

To be of good courage in the face of personal loss or adversity seems beyond the capacity of those who doubt survival, with happier times ahead. Courage is not stressed enough in the Christian outlook. It is essential, together with the knowledge that light will vanquish darkness in Providence's good time.

The deep well provided by the C.W.T. is to be sunk in a village in the Province of Bihar, and I hope may be the first of a series, given by those who gain peace and vision in our Upper Room.

On another tack: some of the questions posed for the P.M. to answer on 'Panorama', BBC 1 on Monday have been provided by WTP. Without clear understanding of the terms of the Treaty of Rome we are being rushed into the position of a mere province of Europe, no longer shall we be masters of our fate. Our standards of morality and ethics are not what they were; but will fall further if and when we become subservient to Europe. (Very few British firms keep two sets of books, one for negotiations over taxation. But this is common practice in most Continental countries.) Today's *Observer* exhorts us to 'Look while you leap'. Would that we had been given the opportunity to look *before* we leap!

And now to a more interesting subject. From time to time in wandering through the immense celestial halls which contain the archives recording the ever-unfolding life on this planet, I have passed on tip toe the doubly sealed entry to a secret chamber.

Recently, I was amazed to see the door ajar, the Guardian absent. So in I went and looked around.

Very soon I realized why this place had remained so very secret during ages of our time. Indeed I wondered whether the door, at long last, had been opened by accident or on purpose? I only glimpsed the contents of the Records within; they were of a kind to revolutionize all our man-made theologies and creeds. Here in full detail was set down a record of the life of Jesus during three incarnations in the era B.C. when he walked the earth as a man, in preparation for the time when he was destined to assume the mantle of the Christos. Revelations of supreme significance, simplicity and purpose, fascinating and inspiring beyond words.

Should my lips be sealed in view of the apparent accident which resulted in my entry to this hidden place?

10.5.67

To continue where I left off: the next time I passed that way the great door was bolted and barred again and the sentinel guarding it entirely uncommunicative. Not that it matters, because once having been inside one can transcend the barriers; but I do not contemplate further intrusion without authority.

One fact I have cleared up to my own satisfaction completely. The dogma of the Virgin Birth is myth. However, the seed of both human parents was infused with a special spiritual quality, or if you prefer theological terms the Holy Ghost descended into the reproductive cells just before conception took place. There was no such miracle antecedent to Jesus' birth on the three earlier occasions: in those instances however his parents had been chosen very carefully.

I have never understood how Jesus could have been equipped to play his great role two thousand years ago with no previous experience of our planetary conditions and the bodily *feel* of a three-dimensional state of being.

174

We have talked glibly about the Akashic Records and left it at that. But come face to face with one fragment of that inconceivably immense Record stored in the universal computer – a register of *facts* alone, no theorizing, no interpretations – then the shock of discovery is immeasurable. These facts have been there, wherever 'there' is, all the time and the computer never ceases to register the truth. If I read it aright, there can be no escape back into the territory of man-made theory and speculation.

Look at the implications for orthodoxy. Peter and Paul, the early Church Fathers, the pre-medieval theologians, have told us *as fact* that (for instance), Jesus was born of a virgin: the computer denies this. That Jesus was God Incarnate, the whole of Divinity embodied in human form – the computer makes it clear that this is fiction. That Jesus was born Man, once for all; now we learn of three previous incarnations. The whole ecclesiastical edifice has been erected on half-truth or sheer falsity. One almost accepts Henry Ford's dictum that history is bunk – even religious history! Where do we go from here?

Give it some thought and then tell me who *you* are! Then perhaps WTP may reciprocate in kind. . . .

The further Dead Sea scrolls about which I spoke to you have now been found. The Israeli Government have them and are haggling with U.S.A. museums. I think their contents will strike a decisive blow at the whole of the 'Christian' theological structure, for which reason they may even be suppressed.

To what extent, one wonders, was Jesus clairvoyant? Did he realize that, far from ushering in the Kingdom, his Church was destined to introduce an era of bloody wars and ruthless cruelty, unparalleled in earlier history? Sometimes one could believe that the world would have been better off without the intervention of what has been miscalled Christianity; or rather, that its arrival was premature by a few thousand years and may have done as much harm as good. Soon after I arrived here and well before the end of last century, I made a report to the Authorities to the following effect: 'Unless you intervene in human affairs in a big way, *and soon*, it is certain that life on this planet will be extinguished.' The reply was somewhat as follows – 'Major issues elsewhere in the solar system must take precedence. The intervention must be called for with real intensity before a response can be expected. It should be available before the end of your next century. Sacrifices resulting from delay will not be forgotten, and will receive compensation.' I have lived my life with this enigmatical utterance ringing in my ears. But I remain an optimist! No doubt the rather dark tone of this screed is partly owing to the fact that it was written during a violent thunderstorm.

18.5.67

Seeking aid towards the expenses of our important C.W.T. digs I have met with no response. The Trustees leave it to WTP to raise the annual sum needed for this work: I am supposed to be quite able to finance these ventures single-handed, and such wishful thinking leaves me rather wry. (Enough of grumbling, I should be thankful for many mercies.)

I feel a little uneasy in having passed on to you in recent letters data that may so easily be misconstrued. It is human to hope that one's thoughts and one's findings should not be swallowed up in the sands of time, so soon as one has gone hence. But it is not for me to write books about the more recondite results of my researches. The following may be repetitive but is related to my recent screeds. Concerning human affairs and Christianity in particular Authority tells me this: 'In planetary matters and also in individual human lives there are occasions when the seeds of progress can only fructify in the womb of failure.' Trial and error? Sometimes it seems that what we deem to be failure is actually

176

engineered from on High. There is more to our experience than meets the eye.

(The re-living of these stupendous events of the past leaves me in suspended animation for days.)

2.8.67

If Mark wrote his own Gospel why should he refer to himself in such an anonymous ambiguous way? It makes no sense. The Young Man was not in Jesus' circle. So far as I know he had never spoken to Jesus before the garden incident, although he had seen him once or twice previously, as a deeply affected onlooker. In those days there were many youths, supposedly deranged, cast out by their families and roaming the countryside. *Our* young man, of course, being a sensitive, was overshadowed for a very special purpose, which included the need for complete anonymity. Bless him!

What a distorted picture of events has come down to us in the New Testament. Of course no one who witnessed (for instance) the writing on the ground, made a written note of what they saw. Perhaps it is a miracle that we have any records at all, incomplete and unreliable as they are. Quite time some seer, better qualified than WTP, went through the whole of the N.T. to clear up the inconsistencies and provide a clear picture of what really happened, and how, and when, during Jesus' earthly Ministry.

9.8.67

Weather good your end? I hope so. Some time send me snaps of all your grandchildren.

By end of the week WTP's notes on some of E.C's queries

should be in typescript. They contain an explanation of the deep purpose lying within Jesus' action in writing on the ground for the *second* time. Watched from two angles, that of the seer and that of the ordinary observer, the same event appeared to be enacted on two separate levels simultaneously, and not identical in pose. Something that always fills me with a strange sense of excitement, and rather rare in my own experience.

Pamphlet enclosed reveals a Canon of the Church of England accepting the tribal God of the Jews, a shockingly autocratic person, as the supreme Creator of the Universe; filled with wrath and jealousy, the inspirer of bloodshed, war and disaster. This curious concept has long been entertained in Christian theology with no recognition of the blasphemy implicit in degrading the God of Infinite Love to such a figure. *Is* there such an all-powerful being as this Jehovah at large in the universe? Rather a disconcerting idea.

18.8.67

The N.T. has now been turned into American of the street corner variety. It is selling by the million, even stocked by drug stores and the big compartment emporia. The demand is there but we who write 'behind the scenes' accounts cannot reach the man in the street.

However, the intelligent semi-believer could be helped, I feel, if Jesus were represented to him less as a God-man than as a very good human being inspired by the spirit of Deity. A man subject to immense stresses which were calculated to break his spirit, and permitted to the point even of risking the failure of his mission (which as a matter of history *did* fail in some important ways). This more realistic appraisal will shock and may even be impossible to get over. But the time has come to attempt the task; and it may perhaps be fruitful among many who stand outside or on the fringe of the Christian (or any other) Faith.

178

I wonder how many who are here today possess personal memories of Jesus when he walked among us? If they exist they are very silent. The many books about Jesus the man are all theory, speculation and supposition. Why is this? I confess that Jesus' attitude following his arrest puzzles me and somehow seems to be out of spiritual focus. Was it that a sense of partial failure made him determined at all costs to fulfil prophecy, to contrive his own death and so convert failure into a measure of achievement? Pilate was ready to save him, but Jesus prevented this by playing on the passions of the Sanhedrin and their cronies. He was deliberately provocative when referring to the destruction of the Temple, and in his outspoken references to himself: and all in terms designed by him to ensure conviction. To the onlooker there seems to have been something almost masochistic in these tactics: one is reminded of the Buddhist monks in India and Viet Nam who set themselves on fire to call attention to political and social wrongs.

Later. Your very satisfying Sunday letter now here and how *good* of you to write when tired out and with so many people milling around. Of course I was *delighted* by the way you spoke and have since heard many who were present echo my feeling. Sally who was there had helped much with the recovery of your voice and seemed keen that you should know this. She had brought musicians and a choir with her and they played in the gardens, and later in the Upper Room. She was so happy to watch you and all you did for the success of the gathering that she did not try to distract your attention, but at the same time made her influence felt in various ways.* Jenny Mills† had been delayed, being on a nursing job, but when she did arrive she helped as a kind of usher among the great unseen concourse attracted for the occasion. Eventually she went off to link her parents and their new home with Chalice Well and the U.R. I have not seen such a large

---

* TP being very unwell, he asked me to read the address he had prepared for Companions' Day at Chalice Well. I had slight laryngitis, and feared that my voice would give out – but instead it became unusually strong and clear!

† Jenny Mills: the only daughter of Ken and Joy Mills, killed tragically on the road in 1965.

gathering since the reception given to Pope John.

Chalice Well's future appears to be a matter of great moment not only to Sally's group but to very wide circles 'up there'. Circles very much concerned with the Jesus and other writings. As to these I am open minded. I cannot judge their value. They were jotted down mostly at times when pain and sweat seemed to dim what I was trying so unworthily to express.

25.8.67

Whilst the orchestra and choir were in action last Saturday I said to Sally that I feared the pitch was too high to be audible even to the most sensitive earthly ear. She then introduced me to the conductor, and I found myself face to face with one of the great musical maestros of all time (ask her about him). He explained that a recording was being made on the etheric counterpart of our atmosphere on wave-lengths that would ensure permanency. And that from these records a stepped-down replica would be made, of a kind which he hoped would create audible echoes, available to be picked up as time passed by many (or some) of the pilgrims able to tune in whilst in C.W. gardens.

The choice of sycamore for the Table is good and only second to olive, and the stools in yew are right. Rigid vegetarians would not be happy for the meal was by no means strictly V! Dried fish soaked in olive oil and served with herb salad and lemon juice. The main dish rice, chicken, wild potatoes, a kind of mushroom, together with a sauce containing 'hot'-flavouring herbs, also mint; all served in a large earthenware dish which stood on the side table, and steaming hot. Apart from Jesus, who was served by the good man's wife, everyone helped himself. Wooden spoons, not knives, were used; a chunk of unleavened bread often replaced a fork, and was eaten (first dipped in salt-water) with the main dish. Dessert consisted of dried figs, nuts, raisins, a kind of guava unknown to me, all served with moist goat's-milk cheese. Wine and cooled drinking water were on the table in smallish jars and pitchers.

After the ceremonial partaking of the bread and wine the cups were rinsed in water before further use. Hands were washed in a large bowl on the side table, before the meal and also between courses and at the end.

Concerning the three denials: Jesus wished to avoid the risk of a mass arrest of his immediate followers, and Peter was used as a focus to divert attention from the rest of the disciples, anyway for the time being. How wrong it is to pass judgement without knowing all the facts!

On a completely separate issue, one which relates to the earthing event; Jesus carried out the anchoring process during the time he spent, after his 'death', in the Underworld (not Hell). This is, literally, the underground area of our planet, the depths of the earth. Here the quickened rhythm which he had earthed previously (in the writing on the ground) was anchored in such a way as to ensure permanency until the next change in frequency should be decreed, which is likely to happen before the present century is out.

Next time you contact Sally ask if *she* knows who that maestro had been on earth.* Many sensitive souls prefer to go forward without disclosing their earth-life identity. I think I shall follow this practice.

Yes a planetary shake-up is one solution but it is not favoured by those who have our planetary Ruler's ear. Their effort is focussed

* I did not discover his identity.

on bringing about drastic changes in man's mental and spiritual outlook.

Jesus' etheric appearances after the Crucifixion were not sufficiently widespread to establish a firm belief in an after life save in a small circle, even though his etheric double became semi-materialized on one or two occasions.

You and E.C. sparked off this current series of notes, and if anything is to be done with them, I think the responsibility rests on your joint shoulders!

3.9.67

Here is the script promised. *Good* of you to find time to come down and see me, or what is left of me here. I am really grateful.

Possibly a title for this small book could be *The Writing on the Ground*? But *you* are the wizard on titles!

With Jesus in the house why should Luke's ministrations to their hostess's little girl have been necessary? (See enclosed script.) Although Jesus rarely if ever used external remedies he was full of lore about herbs and plants, and knew their beneficial effects when properly used. In any case he was a natural healer through his eyes and the touch of his hands.

Enjoy the music and the drama, without which I now feel very much the poorer. Potted music and plays are a sad substitute.

My love as *always*.

Tomorrow will be . . . *14.9.67*

How much I hope you are feeling better and able to enjoy the children and the Island. Out of the blue P.M. popped in and asked when your book would be out and sent you his fond love. (He is learning the right lessons fast but is not yet entirely free from purgatorial regrets.) I suppose we shall all realize our inadequacies and our missed opportunities when we depart?

I have (largely) slipped out of the twentieth century and am living in about 600 B.C.; the first century A.D., and in the twenty-first. Human nature does not seem to change, very hard to see any progress

Sally's passing was the night of your despair. It was also the darkness before dawn, because from her passing began your sunrise of enlightenment. If the Swan, amongst much else, symbolizes the gracious peace of renewed vision then Sally's departure led you forward and upward. Here was no swan at eventide but the Swan of the Dawn, the Swan of the Morning, the Swan of Sunrise.*

I sent you a typescript which gave the bare historical facts about our 'Cup' and disclaimed suggestions that it could be identified with the Grail. It is the symbol of a New Age, and it undoubtedly bears the auric influence associated with Jesus. Publicity might destroy this influence. Pre-Christian Glastonbury is a veiled story, a very long one, far beyond my present capacity to compile or set down. These recent Jesus scripts must be my swan song (but a song of the morning and not of the night).

I once thought of recording my own B.C. experiences in Britain and at Avalon but was advised 'Now now'. Surely some impetus will be given to the next generation to follow up and complete what I have begun. Too much should not be asked of any one pioneer.

---

* These various swans are quite irrelevant in the context of my choice of title: *The Swan in the Evening*! The words appear in a song (old Irish) which Sally used to sing. The song is called *She Moved through the Fair* and somehow evokes her symbolically and subtly in more ways than one.

Jesus said the Spirit could only come if and when he went away. In a miniature and modest sense, much that WTP could impart will be made available as and when he departs; not in the form of communications but in a form that can be picked up by those who care to be receptive and open-minded. Meanwhile is there anything really *important* (to you) that needs elucidation?

Last Sunday a group of 'flower' folk invaded C.W. gardens. They did no harm but the press published the story with pictures of Chalice Well; and we are trying to make it clear that the C.W.T. dissociates itself from cults of all kinds.

Divine Love Creates the Law

The primary laws on which the Universe is based stand forever inviolate and fixed, although their application in external realms of illusion appears to human sense to be subject to fluctuation and chance. No simple answers can be given to your questions, involving as they do knowledge and understanding beyond the reach of man where he stands today. The Will of the First Cause, Whom we call 'God', can seem to be delayed or even defeated within time/space conditions; but even here this Will is fulfilling itself, utilizing for the purpose all our failures, sins and misuse of freewill.

This freedom of the human will is of course very partial in its scope, being subject to the law of cause and effect and also to overruling Providence which says to man, 'Thus far and no further', when the inclination is to plunge into the darkness and destroy himself. As I have said elsewhere, the ultimate object of the Creator is to see Himself reflected perfectly in His Creation. We cannot envisage what this means, but we need to accept as truth the statement that 'All things work together for good'. Yes, with or without our co-operation. Such goodness lies a long way from our faintest power of comprehension.

You may well ask: 'How for instance can the "Fall" of life into matter serve the purposes of Deity?'

There is no solution of this mystery unless by an immense effort of faith we accept 'all things' at face value. In our own lives we witness from time to time what we call good emerging out of what we feel to be evil: this may give us some conception of the working of Providence on the grand scale.

To be more specific in answer to your questions, once a man has become an individual soul his destiny lies *directly* and personally within the control of primary Law. He can resist the Law, but the Law uses his very struggle through which to fulfil itself. As man goes on his way there may be a dozen or more roads which would take him from A to B. He has freedom of choice within the limits of his karmic commitments. The chosen transit may be short or long, easy or very difficult, but it lies outside his power *not* to arrive at B in the end. In the meantime he is subject to the Law of attraction and repulsion, a kind of gravitational process which cannot be evaded. Until a state of Initiateship is reached he cannot choose his parents, or the periods when he will incarnate, here or elsewhere. Without his volition he gravitates to the environment best suited to his karmic needs. We only become Masters of our Fate when self-centred selfishness is replaced by acceptance – 'They Will be done, not mine.' And this is the first doorway.

If after this inadequate attempt at explanation you feel you are a puppet, a convict in shackles, then it is clear that I have failed. The word Love is to be used warily, for our notions fall far short of the reality: but with supreme faith one may begin to realize that supreme and omnipotent Love lies behind and within the Law and all its operations.

I tried to touch the fringe of this subject in the leaflet *God is Love* and I do not know how better to express my own conception of the way in which Love created Law, and how Law will ensure our ultimate salvation.

30.9.67

An international Bahai affair is on at their Temple of Peace in Frankfurt. I am appealed to for personal memories of Abdul Baha 'as the only Westerner now alive who knew him intimately'. (What it is to be an ancient of days!)

In 1911 in my Clifton home A.B. held the Cup in his hands for a very long time, saying nothing. Then he blessed it reverently and gave it back to me.

Sad in my view that the movement is crystallizing into a new religion with hierarchies, temples etc. It should have developed along Quaker lines.

2.10.67

My sister is helping me to clear up masses of papers and oddments. She reminded me of a pleasant story about our Uncle Tom Wansbrough. After the first War, in which he earned the M.C. and the Croix de Guerre, he took a remote farm in Algeria and lived there alone, save for his two beloved wolfhounds, for protection, and a couple of native labourers. After some years the dogs were killed in an accident, a terrible blow to him and a source of great loneliness. Two years later still our Uncle Tom was murdered, killer never traced, murdered for the gold fillings in his teeth.

Six months later my mother had a sitting with Mrs. Osborne Leonard. Our uncle (her brother) made his presence known, and in good spirits. He told her: 'I don't know what happened but I had no reason to think I was "dead" until my two beloved dogs came leaping towards me in a turmoil of joy.' From what he added it was evident that all three were living together in full and happy possession of their lives.

4.10.67

The persona (mask) or bodily personality of the individual fades away when any particular incarnation is over. The essence of the individual and his experiences are drawn back into the parent ego.

186

There are not a row of characters from the past sitting aloft when a fresh incarnation takes place. When someone says, 'I was so-and-so in a past life', and if true, then the personality of that so-and-so no longer exists as such but has become reabsorbed. The ego rarely incarnates as a whole, until Initiateship is reached, but it overshadows very closely the 'person' actually in incarnation; so much so with evolved individuals that they can be said to be acting in integration.

Ability to remember past lives is not necessarily a sign of advanced evolution, just as the faculty of clairvoyance may be available to quite simple souls. Your and my meetings have been rare 'here below' but we have often crossed each other's paths elsewhere, over the ages.

On average about one seventh of most people's time is spent on earth and six sevenths between incarnations, but this proportion is in no way fixed. If your query is not yet answered, let me know.

Troops of people have arrived, strangers. So no more now. My children come when invited but I am no burden to them.

7.10.67

By the way do not feel a sense of separateness between your present conscious self and your ego. At times, perhaps when you are stretching out towards Sally or some distant friend on earth, you will suddenly feel that *you* are much more than your conscious self. A sense of wholeness will begin to emerge, a feeling of authority, of wider horizons, even of power and ability to achieve great things. 'Overshadowing' is not the right word, because you and your greater self are one and can never be divided. The principle of rays is by no means adequate to explain the fundamental unity of the whole self. This contains, of course, the *essence* of all the personalities you have assumed over the long past, both in physical incarnation and elsewhere. Were you once the Queen of Sheba then everything worthwhile in qualities and

187

experiences and in feelings that once were hers is in your possession now and always will be. Naturally the unfoldment of *conscious* possession of your whole self is a very gradual process.

27.10.67

These recent sightings do not seem to come from planetary space, but from our own planet's interior spheres. It *looks* like a missionary effort but does not originate from any source with which I am in touch. Puzzling, but spiritual awareness on the grand scale does not emerge apparitionally and so we can but wait and see. . . .

Tell me if there is anything I can do for you whilst you are in hospital, and of course *any* time. Where will you be? Let your correspondence slide and many letters will then answer themselves. I *try* to practise what I preach!

27.10.67

I was beginning to think that my little genie had retired, or departed elsewhere and in any case, as you know, I never dream of summoning him to my needs. If I did his freewill might be endangered, moreover it would be a descent on my part into a form of magic. My problem, not imparted to him therefore, has been to try to recover from the past data (prior to 1925) to augment my memories of personal contacts with Abdul Baha, his times and teachings. Part 2 of the new book is to be concerned with a comparison of the way truth is revealed at two points in history – in the first days of Christianity, and two thousand years later by Baha Ullah. The relevant records were destroyed when my Duke Street offices were bombed in 1943. The task seemed hopeless; until suddenly my genie popped up with an offer of help, scorning my lack of faith. Things began to happen . . . a useful remnant of a half-bombed file ex Duke St. emerged from a long disused bureau drawer, wedged hidden at the back. And from one of the crates of files stored at Markinch, buried among a mass of letters and rubbish, appeared three invaluable scripts dating back to the early twenties. A very unexpected ally jumped out of the blue in the person of Lord Wakehurst, now Governor of Northern Ireland. The value of this renewed contact is that it has revived memories that had entirely gone to sleep.

Curious that M.L.G. will never say how he works. He brushes gratitude aside. When I lose something of value, his intervention does not seem to depend on my own wishes in the matter, and may or may not be forthcoming. If I were to plead urgency, I doubt I should ever see him again, and thus a wonderful pal would be gone forever.

30.10.67

The Little People spring from the vegetable kingdom. My little fellow comes from the trees. Others emanate from grass and herbs. They are under the control of the V.K's hierarchy. They form two classes – pixies and gnomes etc., the Little People proper: and the more etherialized entities we know as sprites and fairies. In soil and minerals another class exist, far more elemental and less developed, not being individualized yet. In air, fire and water still other elemental forms, which would take too long to describe now. My great love for trees may have first attracted M.L.G. to me. He knows that this contact with me helps him on his way to a greater measure of development and intelligence. But he does not like to feel the need to acknowledge any indebtedness. Bless him and prosper him nevertheless.

Before launching the Silent Minute late in 1939, I stormed (solus) the citadel of Heaven. See enclosed Memo. The value of the response cannot be estimated, but by 1943 over ten million were keeping the 'Minute' on earth and more than double that number elsewhere. Now I am storming the citadel again, and this

189

time I am lucky to have a very reliable channel. We shall see what we shall see, but in any case the rest of my present life on earth, at least, will be devoted to this Quest and to making the *call* imperative. Join in.

2.11.67

Late in 1939 when WTP began to storm the gates of Heaven for a special purpose, the plan he had in view was placed before Authority. The promise then made to him amounted to this: If you carry out your intention to the full we can make this assurance, that a sheath of protection will be arranged rendering invasion of your Island and its subjection impossible. The war itself will be shortened by at least two years.

The story of how invasion by sea was averted has never been told fully, but the fact could be classed as a miracle. The shortening of the war, if it really took place, can never be proved. *Moral:* We should never underestimate the potential value of effort, even by single individuals, in launching a worthwhile spiritual activity. This is a lesson every one of us should take to heart. We should cease to behave like insects, milling around our own little middens, eyes on the ground. We are sons and daughters of God. We should look UP, claim our heritage and enjoy it.

Therefore say to yourself, 'I am a child of God and am able to play my full part in service to my community and to life on this planet in every form. Here and now I dedicate myself anew, prayerfully and free from self-centred desires, in the sure knowledge that one with God is a *majority*.'

6.11.67

I suppose WTP is up to something that displeases our friends on the left. A ferocious elemental attack took place, using a violent burst of wind to hurl the windows and window frames of my sitting room right across the front garden. Nine in the evening, all the lights went out and the room filled with hail stones. Miss W. was very plucky, but Kippy was scared out of his wits by something supernatural. WTP became soaked to the skin trying to retrieve the windows, and in nailing up some mattresses to shut out the wind and the rain, by the light of one candle. I thought that attacks of this kind, so many of which I have survived, were things of the past, but evidently not. . . .

9.11.67

What Kippy saw on the night of the attack I can only surmise, but it gave him such a heart attack that we despaired of his life for several days. He is not yet normal.

I have to spend much time *au delà* just now and it can be a strain, living in two worlds while doing one's job *properly* in both.

24.11.67

I am more than grateful to you for undertaking the trying chore of going through and advising on those scripts.* Your suggestions and help are *invaluable*. The book is going to be altogether rather a *mélange*, but perhaps it will go down passably.

So pleased that your book is going so well. Splendid. I feel that it is bound to do good. You show real courage in revealing so much of the intimate side of your thoughts and feelings, and you have done so in an unselfconscious and modest way.

* *Writing on the Ground.*

Memo: The newly established supra-terrestrial University of Research. This project is now becoming interplanetary, no longer solely concerned with a study of more satisfactory methods of communication between our planet and the spheres surrounding it. The somewhat crude methods current during the past hundred years in particular have allowed a very mixed inflow of forces into human consciousness, good bad and indifferent, the total effect of which is not considered to be of a kind that should persist indefinitely. The Energies of the Left have made far too much use of phenomenal spiritualism, via such channels as ectoplasmic materializations, hypnotism, and in some cases the practice of automatic trance mediumship when undertaken without proper safeguards. It is evidently felt that the time has come to find surer and safer ways for the passage of inspiration. But whilst those who are organizing the activities of this University are closely concerned with this matter (and are seeking a *point d'appui* on our planet as an external anchorage), far wider operations are now under survey.

These include harmonizing and readjusting the etheric and magnetic currents as they play between all the planets of our system, in the interests of all forms of life now evolving on earth.

For the discerning, the following data about the planet Venus may be useful. Astro-physicists tell us that this planet is incapable of sustaining life. On the contrary Venus is a womb in which enbryonic life in many forms is in process of incubation; primary, unindividualized life, being exposed over immeasurable periods of time to cosmic fertilization. (As for too many humans love is equated with sex and fertility, so Venus has come to be regarded as the planet of 'love'.) Venus therefore provides primitive life-forms that pass into our own planet's mineral structure and proceed from there up through the Kingdoms of Nature and finally enter the Kingdom of Man. Venus supplies other planets of our system similarly, and in accordance with the evolutionary purposes of the planet concerned.

However, what is of moment to humanity at present is that its seers should take heed of the developments touched upon earlier in these notes, and through prayer, meditation and conduct co-operate in the thinning of the veil; so that new inspiration and healing, urgently needed, may reach our sadly stricken world.

All went well on Monday, and the Upper Room has now taken on an almost supernatural and strangely pervasive atmosphere. The table is finely proportioned, with a lovely sycamore top, and the stools of yew are completely right. M. Baly took especial care in carving the Master's stool (the only one with a back rest). Present: Mr. and Mrs. Baly, two of their craftsmen, Joy Mills, Kenneth Cuming, Chris Langlands and the Simmons. So soon as the furniture had been arranged and the party had retired for lunch, an impressive little ceremony took place, during which the Custodian of the Room was installed by an Elder Brother amidst an impressive concourse, comprehensive beyond my expectations. Evidently more is on foot than meets mortal eye. Nice that *you* were (are) in on all this.

For the first time in memory the thorn trees in the gardens are in bud, bloom and fruit simultaneously; the flowering being four weeks earlier than usual. A coterie of large brown hares came down into our orchards and these shy lovely creatures were, I am told, completely free from fear. This has never happened before. Birds were singing and the sun was shining.

The triad of spirit, mind and body is mis-named the 'Eternal Triangle'. Body is not eternal by any means. When time is absorbed in a higher dimension, then matter will disappear *for good*. This Triangle would be better constructed of spirit, mind and form, because spirit will continue to clothe mind in form indefinitely, even if such form be entirely devoid of matter and if it assume attributes far beyond our present comprehension.

This cattle plague is karmic. We have disturbed the balance of nature by poisoning the soil and soil life, by using animals for vivisection, and by the cruelties of artificial insemination and the penning of poultry etc., into confined spaces. Will man never learn? I know of several farmers in the stricken areas whose livestock has remained immune. In each case the farmer and his hinds have an almost brotherly love and understanding for the animals in their care.

You have gathered a mass of WTP material which when sifted could throw light on this and many other problems. Don't let it run to waste. After my withdrawal, receptivity to much of this data will become more and more widespread. I am very unlikely to come this way again for a very long time: needs elsewhere must be met.

Bless you and all you do and are.

18.12.67

I hear rumours of a young fellow in Indonesia, who is said to possess the faculty for personal research in those regions which lie above Borderland and the astral levels. I am trying to contact him but do not know his name and address. It would be wonderful to compare notes with a first-hand researcher into those higher realms which, to a large extent, control conditions here and in Borderland. Literature abounds in hearsay, messages from lately departed people, most of whom know little more than we do about the reality above and behind the illusory. Has any Westerner recorded his experiences in the way this Indonesian is reputed to have done? Did Cayce go high enough to do so?

22.12.67

What a lovely letter and present has come from you! They brought a renewed glow of gratitude for your loyal and affectionate companionship and for your selfless support in dealing with various problems and vicissitudes. Your handling of the *Messenger of Chalice Well* galleys was salutary, salubrious and I might almost add, sanitary. Oh for less gush about 'God' and 'Love'. These two words have become prostituted beyond all bounds.

Thank Providence that the obstruction between the spring's underground source and the well shaft has now been spotted (twenty feet below ground) and rectified.

My sister Kitty is here and longing to read your book. How grateful you must be for its enthusiastic reception. Even five years ago understanding of its contents would have been far from general, and it might even have roused animosity.

29.12.67

No one will credit it, but the blue sapphire bowl spent most of Christmas 'elsewhere', and was present in the Upper Room at Glastonbury on Christmas Eve during lovely music and unearthly harmonies then manifesting. Fiona Macleod (William Sharpe) forecast an illumined future for Avalon; and, I believe, perceived a great destiny for the Cup. But *what*? And is that destiny linked with the denouement of the Quest in Stamboul?!

Haste for post. *Bless* you in 1968.

31.1.68

How very trite it is to assure the bereaved, the sufferers from the suicide of loved ones, that to know all is to forgive all. The suicide reference in *The Silent Road* might help your correspondent, whose bitter sorrow has closed the avenue that her beloved has been trying for so long to open and use. I don't suppose she would understand the workings of Karma. This brilliant young man suffered unknown from a growth on the brain; and I think he suspected that in any case his departure could not be long delayed. His grandfather met and solaced him, helped him through his purgatory and put him on his feet. Selfless love inspired by Divinity is a power of immense strength, far reaching and capable of miraculous achievements. This fellow is strong and well,

195

training for valuable work, free now from the effects of his act; striving to reach and console his mother, and preparing a happy place for her when her time comes. Help her to destroy the barriers of her own creation.

6.2.68

I often think how much better equipped to face life *self-reliantly* is the Buddhist youth reared in a cultured family, say in Ceylon, than his western counterpart brought up on public school Christianity. The former is taught to regard the founder of his Faith as an elder brother, accessible through meditation, friendly and compassionate; not to be regarded as a Saviour, to whom worship must be directed and petitions for 'salvation' made. Such a youth realizes that the Lord Buddha, being as subject to the Law of Cause and Effect as he is himself, has no power to wipe away sins and obliterate evil. That therefore the need to crawl worm-like, in search of forgiveness and salvation, does not exist; that he alone is master of his fate, in that he must return to earth until a measure of perfection has been reached. Reared on Christian theology, lacking the same understanding and sense of personal responsibility, the western youth seems to be at a disadvantage all down the line. Heresy! But how tragically Christian teaching has missed its mark!

10.2.68

For some time past now I have limited what one might call the professional use of my own Upper Room (and the Cup) to one patient at a time. Since before Christmas the focus has been on a courageous and attractive lad of seventeen (Richard C. of Belfast). Six months ago he was struck down by cancer in the bones of his left leg, with the lungs also affected, and the end seemed near. My part has been to supervise the small local (Irish) healing group, amateurs but faithful. The Watcher in Chalice Well's Upper Room was brought in indirectly, as a consultant so to speak, but WTP does not wish to stress the value of his own modest part in this combination of helpers; the Watcher *diverted* my work and attention altogether from the bodily conditions, the terrible external symptoms, spreading so fast and seemingly beyond control. Concentration was set upon the karmic conditions and the possibility that *these* could be transmuted and short-circuited. One never knows for certain (anyway I don't!) when such intervention can be allowed to the point of real effectiveness. What interests me is how far the Cup's aura can be used in cases like this (and so become an important healing factor when it is permanently transferred to C.W. from my small sanctuary. Who can be trained to follow this up when the time comes? Why so far has it only been allowed to use it in this way so rarely? I have never attempted, for instance, to use it for the thorn in my own flesh. Why not, I wonder? Karmic again, or that I don't care enough for matters of this kind affecting myself? Here is a good example of WTP's limitations of vision in respect of himself.)

A few days ago all pain ceased, swellings disappeared, X-rays showed a complete arrest of the disease, lungs cleared, and the youngster actually got up, went out and drove a car from the clinic to his home, five miles away. For once the surgeons and specialists can offer no explanation and have made no attempt to conceal their complete bewilderment. The cancer diagnosis was correct beyond all doubt. The family's G.P., without much conviction, says that one case in ten thousand of this kind of cancer has been known to clear up spontaneously and incomprehensibly. The cure is not yet complete and no doubt the possibility of a relapse cannot be ruled out. But it is as if the power of the Christos had touched and healed this lad, and one wonders if the channel for this touch passed through the aura of our blue sapphire bowl? Is Chalice Well and its Upper Room (and this vessel) destined to initiate a new dispensation of healing, based on the methods which Jesus made his own? One hardly dares even to ask this question. Meanwhile the few whom J.S. allows to visit the C.W. Upper Room speak of their experiences there with awe and upliftment.

I think the Pope was very wrong in encouraging human organ transplants. The karmic and other effects are very dangerous.

The American defeat in Viet Nam and their home troubles remind one of the prophecies made in 1916 in *Private Dowding* about the coming of tribulations upon U.S.A. It seemed unlikely then for the richest and most powerful country on earth. Realization is now dawning that dollars in profusion cannot solve all the problems of man. Quite time that our Elder Brothers acted decisively if they really want to avert a very grave setback in human evolution.

Enquiries pour in from people worried about transplantation of human organs. Artificial surgery of this kind may prolong life but it is *not* evolutionary, in the spiritual sense.

The etheric double of the departing soul is not affected by the transfer of an organ or organs from the body of that soul to someone still living – living in the physical sense. The latter however may become subject to dislocation of his or her own auric and etheric vibrations, not always beneficially: the magnetic sheath which surrounds and cushions the physical body, and disintegrates with that body, is *not* a portion of the etheric double so is not withdrawn, and that part of it associated with a living organ remains with the organ when the latter is transplanted into another living body. 'Life' may or may not be prolonged, but mental and psychical conditions can be disturbed as a result.

Meanwhile the etheric double of the donor remains intact as the overcoat used by the departing soul in preparation for its new vehicle of manifestation, usually called the astral or body of light. During the change the grosser elements of the etheric disintegrate, but its finer elements are absorbed into the astral form, one that is far more 'solid', versatile and harmonious than the physical body that has been left behind.

We mumble and grumble to each other about our burdens of massive correspondence. In your case the problem has been accentuated through the brilliant success of your new book. Imagine the alternative: the book a frost, and no letters about it! Preferable?

By the way I should have made it clear in mine of yesterday that surgery cannot tamper with, nor reach, the etheric counterpart of the body or any organ in it. When an organ is transplanted its etheric double remains unmoved in the vacuum resulting, being an integral portion of the whole etheric structure which is an entity, so to speak, in its own right. There are no physical cells or atoms in this etheric body therefore neither fire (cremation) nor sword (surgery) can touch it. People write me in panic about the question, having no conception of a four-dimensional structure.

It is evident that the blue sapphire bowl possesses a life and individuality of its own. And an unseen Guardian. *So far* and since 1906 there has been need for a watcher on earth to act both as custodian and as interpreter of the wishes of the Guardian (and perhaps those of beings higher up). When and if this vessel is deposited in the 'Upper Room', the Chalice Well Trustees will become responsible for it: who among them is equipped to act in the capacity hitherto the province of WTP? Or is the Cup's final resting-place to be somewhere else? Important decisions as to its future functions, especially in relation to the general public, cannot be long delayed. Is the solution that it should be returned to the waters as near as possible to St. Bride's Well (no longer in existence) where it came to light in 1906?

Yesterday evening, having had the question of the Cup much in mind, I set off for bed realizing that efforts were being made to obstruct the outcome. On reaching the first bend of the staircase I was met by a blast; lifted up and flung down into the hall below. It was clear that the intention was to expunge me bodily before certain events could transpire. Miss W. picked me up, semiconscious, black and blue but no bones broken. Temporarily my mind was rendered completely blank beyond the knowledge that the Cup's destiny was in the balance and that it was imperative to call up reinforcements instantly. All I could do, then, was to call for the passing of the danger that we were at the end of the chapter for the Cup.

What great issues must be involved for the Left to come out into the open so forcibly at this particular juncture! One thing is certain, or almost so – had it not been for the recovery of the Cup in 1906 Avalon and Chalice Well would still lie supine in the shadows, impotent to play their part in the reawakening of Britain and her people to their spiritual destiny. Humbling to realize that a supposedly inanimate object can play the stupendous role of focus for the manifestation of such an event?

I think I told you that years ago blood was transfused into my body at a time when life was ebbing. I was then outside my body, walking in the moonlit garden of the nursing home in Tunbridge Wells. I had no intention of returning, until an unseen bell began insistently to toll and gave me no choice. I then found that the 'I am' had tackled the intruder successfully to bring about harmonious absorption. The problems can be surmounted but the road to spiritual progress does not lie in these directions.

WTP's spine and neck creak and cringe, but why is his neck not broken and have done with it? I am embarrassed by the provision of two sentinel/detectives, now never absent. One might be

Royalty or a Cabinet Minister. No privacy! Not angels by any means but two fine workers, seconded from their invaluable work in Borderland, and both well known to me: Private Dowding, now fully integrated, well trained and no longer a retiring sensitive acolyte; the other, Jack Cheape, whose story I may never have told you? His father being married beyond redress to another than the boy's mother, I was partly for this reason Jack's guardian throughout his schooldays. A lad of immense promise, very fully the Stephen type, he went into the army in 1914 and was killed in 1915 in Flanders. His mother lingered and then departed broken-hearted. Now he is a valiant warrior, braving fearlessly the leftish influences in Borderland and a splendid ally, but by no means what one would call a saintly or angelic character. Otherwise he (and P.D.) could not carry on their mission successfully in very dark regions. Doubtless they will both be on duty when you and B. come down.

27.3.68

One should not distort the perspective of history to satisfy individual tastes and beliefs. Are we asked to delete the passage in question and to replace it by an historical falsity? If so, then much of *A.M.S.A.* and *W. on the G.* might as well be re-written. To lower the standard of truth for fear of giving offence would serve an ignoble purpose.

WTP, or whoever it was who recorded those events was a passer-by, inhabitant of a world far removed from Hebrew orthodoxy or the social and religious milieu which formed the background for Jesus' short life in human form. Here was a man of deep simplicity, of transparent goodness yet capable at times of intemperate words and actions, a political revolutionary whose vision embraced the centuries and beyond; and yet one who anticipated the fulfilment of his visions within a single generation of human time. From an onlooker versed in the philosophies of the ages, the description 'a great seer' was high praise indeed.

Undoubtedly this observer was deeply moved by the comparatively casual encounters with Jesus that came his way. His thoughts and feelings about this Master's true spiritual status were not of a kind to be worn on the sleeve. In previous epochs there had been somewhat similar contacts with Masters who also, in their time and way, were manifestations of the eternal principle of the Christos. (Destiny had been kind in this respect, and no doubt purposeful.) Are we, today, really capable of judging the comparative status of Avatars, to the extent of asserting that Jesus was the greatest manifestation of the Logos who has ever trod the earth? Or ever will? A wise man who knew and followed Baha Ullah placed him, spiritually speaking, above Jesus. But such comparisons are offensive and quite uncalled for. The Christos incarnates in myriad ways great and small, and although I should place its manifestation through Jesus at the highest level I am able to conceive of, this is not to say that my judgement is necessarily correct.

However all this is far too ponderous to be passed on to our worthy critic. What you said in yours to me will do admirably. The marvel is that we have not been deluged with abuse. Is this because our generation has lost its religious fire and feeling? Or because after all truth shines forth with subtle persuasion from our pages?

19.4.68

My very dearest A., no need to feel regret. It is far better to let off steam than compress it, so long as one selects the understanding friend for this healing or relieving process. Alas that I am far too prone to let off steam on you!

History does repeat itself. My very close friendship with W. Lady Paget became harried by the attempts of jealous outsiders to drive a wedge between us. I detect similar activity now in relation to you and me. 'Friends' mutual to us strive to disillusion me in devious ways, but of a kind very easily spotted, regarding yourself; it cuts no ice, but is a sad sign of what insensate jealousy can do. Useless to be diverted or to lose serenity of mind and spirit. The Left can be very clever in the instruments they use . . . and now to pleasanter topics! Yes we must provide a quiet reading and talking room at Little St. Michael. A very important conference in high spheres was in progress on Maundy Thursday, connected with intervention and how much of this could be sanctioned and through whom. A messenger from this conference came down whilst you were up in the Upper Room and I gather that Chalice Well is to have its vital part to play.

I should not mention it and have not done so to anyone, but I was allowed to know that Jesus himself was overshadowing (or lighting) what was going on, whilst the four of you were up there. I wish I could speak about his present mission both here and hereabouts. . . .

Martin Luther King. He was told about his imminent departure and accepted it, but did not know the way in which the end would come. He was a seer and very selfless, and he asked that the sacrifice of his earthly life would be used to forward the cause for which he had striven. In a way, there was a parallel between Jesus' 'death' and his own, in that he can now do far more for his people than by lingering on here he could have achieved. Here was a case where the manipulations of the Left were used for good. How *can* we mere humans expect to comprehend the ways in which evil serves cosmic ends? M.L.K. is now gathering together a concourse of martyred negroes over there, and their influence on the earthly scene will prove of immense importance and healing value. This campaign may meet with chemicalization, but no matter, for Light will begin to emerge from the darkness.

2.5.68

Lines of Communication
Concern continues to grow among our Elders, those who help to guide human destiny, about what we may call the short-circuiting of the 'cable' connexions which link us with the wider realms

around us. Evidence of dislocation is seen in the way messages and teachings from higher levels are at times distorted and thus seriously misinterpreted. The premature and artificial manner in which so many millions of men and women have been thrust out of incarnation, long before their time, during this past half-century, may well be one of the main causes of the congestion by which the lines of psychic communication have become entangled. We have seen an instance of the dangerous way in which transmission can be interfered with in the instance of those messages received through psychic channels, during the past five or six years, purporting to come from a very high source, and proclaiming the imminent arrival on our shores of a Messenger from God: in some quarters interpreted as referring to Jesus the Christ, supposed to be returning to earth, and in *bodily* form. These messages have been broadcast around the world, the date for the event having been confidently predicted for Christmastide 1967.* Is it any wonder that such distortions of truth have caused deep anxiety among those whose mission it is to guide humanity forward along the path of orderly evolution? I do not wish to be misunderstood. It is far from my intention to condemn so many spirit communications, linking the seen with the unseen, that continue to be received through mediumship automatically and otherwise. Such messages, bringing solace to the bereaved, have done and are doing much to destroy the fear of the illusion we call 'death'. It is evident, however, that the time is ripe for the gradual upliftment of human consciousness from the level of phenomenal communication to that of spiritual communion, such as we might describe as metaphysical telepathy, mind meeting mind irrespective of time, space or dimension. From time immemorial saints, initiates and many far less evolved individuals have attained this goal, through prayer, meditation and silence. For them, no lines of communication are necessary and the risk of misinterpretation ceases to exist. This is the way to awaken and bring to our aid the Christ within. If the call for succour now being so urgently voiced by mankind brings a response, then we may indeed expect the arrival of a Teacher or Teachers in our midst to show us the way from communication to communion.

* 'Weeping Angel' prediction was actually for an unspecified date *before* Christmas '67.

Meanwhile I am by no means alone in observing the establishment in intermediate regions of a University of Research to deal with the whole problem of the cleansing of the spheres, and also for the purpose of instituting new conditions for the thinning of the veil, *with safety*. Our co-operation is asked for, perhaps, in the establishment of *points d'appui* or focal centres; for use as links between the third- and fourth-dimensional conditions of being.

Many thinkers will reject the notion that any need exists outside our own world for such a University. They may well argue that the cosmic Plan for the human race is already inviolate in all respects. The idea that the Creator and all the Company of Heaven are involved in the evolutionary process must be strange and abhorrent to theologians, as to the ordinary man. But to all who accept the belief that the Creator, through Christ, resides within all forms of life everywhere, then the principle of evolution must surely apply to the gods as well as to us mere mortals?

A.M.S.A. Your correspondent confuses Jesus with the eternal Christ, for whom Jesus became the mouthpiece for about three years. In a certain sense this Christ principle did temporarily individualize in Jesus. The words 'Before Abraham was, I am', did not refer to Jesus but to the Christ speaking through him. Certainly Jesus remembered details of many of his own previous earth lives, which did include incarnations around the times of the early Hebrew prophets, but he was not one of them.

What may be called his incarnations of preparation, mainly in the Far East, ranged from princely status to farmer, mountaineer, recluse and saintly healer, and on one such visit to our planet Jesus was an elephant boy in India and later a tamer of lions, tigers and leopards for an Indian ruler. The supposition that he has never incarnated again in two thousand years is, in my view, incorrect. *If* you decide to quote me, make it clear that I claim no authority whatever for what I say and that dogma is anathema to WTP.

15.6.68

The asteroid Icarus now within five million miles of earth is believed to be a break-away from a former planet situated between Mars and Venus. Its orbit being eccentric is not easy to gauge, but Icarus comes nearer every nineteen years or so. Astronomers won't comment on the astrologers' view that this is or was the Star of the Magi. Certainly its comparatively close approach now is causing certain ferments in our magnetic atmosphere, and may perhaps have reactions on the saucer phenomena. The latter activities do not excite me wildly.

The fellow officer who smuggled home a letter from me to the Cabinet about Abdul Baha's danger in March 1918 was the present Lord Harlech's father, then the Hon. D. Ormsby Gore. To evade the censorship, to bypass Allenby and the W.O. and also to scout official consent, would have made us subject to court martial if found out. D.O.G's action was a link in the chain which saved A.B. and his family from death. On p. 153 of *W. on the G.* I give the facts but mention no name.

17.6.68

Memo
The rescue of Abdul Baha. Chain of events.
February 1918. WTP, then on the Intelligence Staff at Cairo, hearing reports concerning Abdul Baha's grave danger, approached Allenby and other military leaders in the Near East but was met with complete and ignorant indifference.
March 1918. WTP decided to evade the very strict censorship, to bypass his military superiors on the spot; also to side-track the War Office in London; and to find means for a direct approach to the British Cabinet (a court martial offence and the sin against the Brass Hats' Holy Ghost). At this juncture Major David Ormsby Gore was in Egypt, as an attaché (for the Foreign Office) to the Zionist Commission then visiting Egypt and Jerusalem. WTP met D.O.G. at the Sporting Club in Alexandria and enlisted his services. As a serving officer he too was subject to King's Regulations and Censorship Control. Nevertheless D.O.G. agreed to carry an uncensored letter from me to London: addressed to Walburga Lady Paget. This he duly did and she passed the letter on to her son-in-law, Lord Plymouth. The latter

took it direct to Balfour who arranged for its contents to be placed on the agenda of a Cabinet meeting, at which were present Lloyd George, Milner, Curzon and Balfour himself. This was followed by a cable direct to Allenby (*not* sent via the W.O.!) which resulted in action being taken as described in *Writing on the Ground*.

21.6.68

I hope the weekend was a success and full of interest. (Or rather, *will* be! for I am writing on a Friday and will post to the I. of W. in due course.) First: banish the feeling that I am indiscreet and pass on what you tell me to anyone. It is true that in writing to you, and you *alone*, discretion is absent, but then I am on very safe ground. Even my own family are quite unaware of anything that is shared with you alone. Apart from a boyish infatuation with La Duse (which still makes me blush), Walburga has been the only other in my life with whom discretion was needless. When her granddaughter Lady Phyllis Bentley sold my private letters to the British Museum I began to destroy all personal correspondence, and do so still.

As to biography, WTP's personality has no value, all that is worth recording is the Message for which he has tried to be a channel and failed rather dismally.

I have been the depository of secrets all my life, political, social and domestic. Not even shared with my wife of forty years, whose love and understanding were precious beyond all count.

Enjoy and relax and become refreshed.

24.6.68

Concerning that photograph of curious cloud formations over Iona: clouds of this description become a reflection of cosmic convolutions, and a seer who examines them very carefully can often interpret what is going on behind the scenes and from his reading predict the effect, of these gyrations of pure cosmic energy, on human and world events. This could become a science in times to come.

28.6.68

Your letter from I. of W. needs a more careful reply than what I have already sent you, but that means boring you with a tediously long screed. I doubt I shall be allowed to enlarge much on the reasons why I am on earth now, and even if put into words these reasons could be misunderstood. The message and not the messenger is really all that matters.

I agree that this robs any biography of what that word signifies and it is only fair to you, in view of your request, that I should raise the curtain a little on my sombre past. . . .

Some forty years ago I was immersed in research into reincarnation, by no means a spiritual pastime. I used, as aids and focal points, Tarot cards, crystal gazing, colour and number computations, hand reading, and no doubt a measure of clairvoyance. I never accepted fees, but, had I turned professional, I could have become rich. £100 per reading was proffered over and over again, mainly from people in society. It became clear that these readings of the past satiated curiosity, created sensation, but *on the whole* did more harm than good. So I gave it all up, leaving a rota of unsatisfied clients, to whom I unwisely promised attention should the way open to resume the task. Most of these have now departed with the flux of time, but I daresay some dozen wait on patiently and hopefully.

30.6.68

The B.B.C. would like my help in preparing a film on the life and work of Padre Pio. A few years ago I would have welcomed such an opportunity, but not now. How pleasant it is to experience direct and loving intervention from *au delà*! A day or two ago, I was in intense bodily agony. My doctor was away and his sub. beyond reach. Another doctor, motoring from Brighton to Haywards Heath, suddenly felt impelled to stop his car (immediately opposite my house) in order to listen in for possible S.O.S. calls. When he heard the S.O.S. he was able to answer the message by saying, 'Right! I happen to be exactly opposite the house whose address you give me.' He turned out to be charming and very efficient and helpful.

11.7.68

Glad to have your report on your trip west. Joy M. has talent in sketching and I am touched by the trouble taken. But photos and sketches of the mortal WTP, so urgently asked for, are anathema to him.

Lord Harlech's people are to do a T.V. half-hour programme on C. Well in the autumn. A pamphlet must be left over *pro tem.* as I have to meet a £200 bill meanwhile for deficits on previous C.W.T. digs.

Ninety per cent of people both in and out of the Church continue to regard God as statically perfect and immutable. The idea that the Creator is *not* a rock, forever fixed, but a moving and evolving island, causes much dismay. Intimations of instability.

My day. 9 a.m. to 11 a.m. Going through the mail and selecting letters that need immediate attention. 11.30 a.m. until 5 p.m. taken up in answering them, before the next batch arriving by second post. Other chores of a similar kind have to be relegated to sleepless nights. I try to keep the early evenings free for callers and for a little meditation or for writing articles or reviews. This sounds like grumbling and somehow, something must give soon.

When do you leave for Portugal? What a lovely break and refresher that will be! (Envious? Yes.)

209

17.7.68

Your vignette about the Canterbury weekend delighted me. Sweet of you to suggest what you do about Portugal. My obligations for August are already overwhelming. For a real holiday I must wait until released 'aloft'. However I was looking at the agenda the other day of tasks urgently awaiting fulfilment *au delà*. They don't suggest any holiday in the offing, although I suppose every day, here or elsewhere, should be a 'holy day' (a wholly day) – holiness in no confining sense, but as an expression of wholeness. We will alert Peter in due course. He still feels remorse when looking back at missed opportunities of service.

Thank you for grooming no. 7 *Chalice Well Messenger*. Despite the welter of fringe publications I think the *M.C.W.* distinctive enough to be kept alive. I am still finding £50 each issue.

I will autograph and provide you with a copy of *W. on the G.*, later. It was fear of sentimentality which prevented my embellishing the frontispiece with the dedication 'To Alexias with my love'. Usually I am allergic to book dedications, and incidentally I am tired of people trying to probe my past for savouries. What *would* they make of Alexias?! I cannot even contemplate the fury that would have engulfed me. . . . Jealousy is a pernicious weed, one outside your own make-up.

6.8.68

I daresay there are priorities which govern the order of release of metaphysical information. I have gone as far as I was permitted in my new book and in any case there must be other writers as well equipped as WTP, or better, to carry the message forward. Of course we are all very impatient and keen to explore further. Deep sleep is the time when the soul can secure the light from within. The human mind cannot run before it can walk, and we are little more than toddlers.

You have been associated with Clarice T. on one or two occasions, but not in the way she visualizes. If only I could get a few days really free I would take another journey into the past. But the present is filled with demanding urgencies. The increased wobble of our planet as it spins round the sun causes concern in instructed quarters, and even I have been called in to play a modest part in attempts at rectification.

P.S.   I find it difficult to understand why the supply of trained workers, both here and above, seems so inadequate. To the point that those who are available are overworked.

May you all be revelling in the sunshine and renewing life in those lovely surroundings. Many thanks for yours. The sun came out just in time to greet the C.W. gathering yesterday. About ninety present, many more being defeated by road congestion. Kenneth C. and Martin I. spoke well, the former read my address. Cynthia L. took the Chair. Your Sally, so much with you, looked in and arranged some magnificent music, played both in the gardens and in the Upper Room. Evidently she sees a fresh phase now emerging in her beloved mother's life. About forty of the new book were sold during the day. Nearly a page long review came out in Barbanell's paper, by one Gordon Turner and very friendly. However he quarrels with my menu for the Last Supper, and regrets no mention of a large silver charger, couches and/or settees etc. Medieval art tried to transform a very humble and simple occasion into a rich and splendid feast in sumptuous surroundings and this reviewer has fallen under the spell.

I have met Nostradamus but not here. He is now a member of the College of Heralds, and so comes my way at Council meetings. These are often held in the unique and lovely herbal garden attached to the College's estate. No use looking into the past to identify WTP with this or that historical figure. I come and go, when summoned so to do, but the human race is not my race. I try *hard* to identify myself with human problems, joys and sorrows when here, with the deepest compassion, but this is not my planet: I am a modest and anonymous ambassador from elsewhere.

These last three sentences, from his last letter to me, make perhaps a fitting conclusion in this correspondence.

R.L.